W9-AEM-572

FAMOUS
AMERICAN NEGROES

Famous Biographies for Young People

325.26
H

FAMOUS
AMERICAN NEGROES

by

LANGSTON HUGHES

Illustrated

D O D D ,   M E A D   &   C O M P A N Y
N E W   Y O R K   *1 9 6 5*

Wingate College Library

COPYRIGHT, 1954, BY LANGSTON HUGHES

All Rights Reserved

No part of this book may be reproduced in any form
without permission in writing from the publisher

Tenth Printing

Library of Congress Catalog Card Number: 54-5985

PRINTED IN THE UNITED STATES OF AMERICA

To

IVAN AND DOROTHY

27094

CONTENTS

INTRODUCTION

THE HISTORY OF THE American Negro, contrary to common belief, did not begin with slavery. There were many Negroes in the Americas who were never slaves. Some of them came to the Western World as explorers. One of the pilots with Christopher Columbus, Pedro Alonso Niño, was, so some historians believe, a colored man. When Balboa discovered the Pacific Ocean in 1513, his expedition included a number of Negroes who helped to clear the first highway from the Atlantic to the Pacific, across what is now the Isthmus of Panama. And, four hundred years ago, there was an African, Estavanico, connected with the earliest written history of the American Southwest. This dark explorer came to the New World with a group of Spaniards who were shipwrecked on the coast of Florida. All but four of them were drowned. These remaining four, including Estavanico, wandered for eight years among the Indians, and eventually travelled as far South as Mexico City. From there, with Friar Marcos de Niza, in 1539 Estavanico set out on an adventurous trek toward the North in search of the Seven Cities of Cibola. These fabled cities of gold they did not find. But when, near the Rio Grande, the Spaniards tired of the desert heat, they sent the Negro on alone with a few Indian runners to bring back reports of what he found. Estavanico discovered and opened up to European settlers what is now the rich area of Arizona. His discovery occurred eighty years before the first slave ship arrived at Jamestown and the custom of selling human beings was established in North America.

From the earliest days of our history not all slaves remained in bondage. Some ran away to freedom—as did the sailor, Crispus Attucks, who died fighting the British at the beginning of the American Revolution. Some slaves were allowed to hire themselves out for wages and so succeeded in working

Introduction

out their purchase price. Others, like the poet, Phillis Wheatley, were granted freedom by their owners. And many like Sojourner Truth, Harriet Tubman, and Frederick Douglass not only escaped themselves, but devoted their lives to freeing others. Certainly before the War between the North and the South, in one way or another, for nearly two hundred and fifty years the lives of all the Negroes in America, free or slave, were affected by slavery. Just as since the War between the States, the lives of colored citizens have been greatly affected by the problems left in its aftermath. Freed without land, money, or education, since Abraham Lincoln signed the Emancipation Proclamation in 1863, the story of the Negro is one continuous struggle upward toward the status of full citizenship. In some parts of our country this goal has not yet been attained, although progress has been tremendous.

The careers of the famous American Negroes in this book were achieved, not only in the face of the handicaps which any other Americans might have, but *in spite of* the additional difficulties which Negro Americans have known —beginning with slavery when a man did not belong to himself but to someone else, and since continuing with such varied racial discriminations as not being permitted to vote, to go to a state university, to draw a book from a public library, buy or rent a house in some localities, or perform on the stages of concert halls in some sections of our United States. Such difficulties in one form or another are an integral part of the handicaps which each individual in this book had to overcome. Yet, with their great strength or great talent, within the flexibility which democracy possesses, they were able to make themselves into unusual men and women. *How* they did it is one part of their story. The *circumstances* under which they did it is another. The two elements cannot be separated if we are to understand what their careers mean both in terms of personal effort and of democratic possibilities.

American democracy has produced the largest group of outstanding Negroes in the world—from the Colonial poet, Phillis Wheatley to the contemporary Pulitzer Prize winner in poetry, Gwendolyn Brooks; from the fearless fighter for freedom a hundred years ago, Frederick Douglass, to the recent champion of the world in the prize ring, Joe Louis; from the great Shakespearean actor of the early 1800's, Ira Aldridge, to such stars

Introduction

of the theater, radio, and screen as Ethel Waters or the late Canada Lee; from distinguished ministers of the slave period like Richard Allen, to Howard Thurman, Dean of the Chapel at Boston University. There have been many famous Negro citizens in our country. They have worked in almost all fields of human endeavor from the sciences to politics, the arts to sports, religion to business. It is my privilege now to write about only a few, but their careers are representative of many others of whom our country may well be proud.

L. H.

PHILLIS WHEATLEY

PHILLIS WHEATLEY

Whose Poetry George Washington Praised

Born about 1753—Died 1784

SHE WAS A frail mite of a child, dark as chocolate, cute, shy, and rather pretty in an exotic African way. There was something about her delicate face and bright eyes that appealed to John Wheatley so, soon after the sails were lowered on the ship that brought her from Senegal, he bought her as a servant for his wife and their twin son and daughter. The little girl's eyes were wide at the busy wonders of a strange new world as Mr. Wheatley led her from the dock through the streets of Boston. But the cobble stones were cold to her bare feet, and the child didn't know where she was going, or whether to laugh or cry.

John Wheatley was a well-to-do tailor and he took the youngster to his comfortable home where she was received with kindness. No one knew how old the girl was but, because she was losing the last of her baby teeth, her mistress thought she must be six or seven. Since the child did not know a word of English, and no one in Boston in 1761 could speak Senegalese, not only the young one's background but even her name remained unknown. So the Wheatleys called her Phillis and gave her their last name, Wheatley. Before the girl was twenty-one this name, Phillis Wheatley, had become famous throughout the Colonies and even in England. This little African slave grew up to become one of the best known poets of her time.

It happened that Phillis had a gentle mistress who, seeing that she was a bright child, soon taught her to read and write. In those days in many parts of colonial America it was against the law, and certainly contrary to custom, to teach slaves to read and write. Nevertheless, by some good fortune, a number of slaves did learn. And some of them, even before Phillis had published her poems, became known as poets. A colored woman named Lucy Terry in Deerfield, Massachusetts, in 1746, wrote, among other verses, *Bars Fight,* a vivid rhymed account of an Indian raid on the town where she lived. Another Negro in bondage, Jupiter Hammond, began publishing poems as broadsides in Queens Village, Long Island, in 1760. And eighteen years later he paid tribute to the Boston slave girl whom he had never met in his *A Poetical Address to Phillis Wheatley.*

When the ship with its cargo of slaves which included the delicate child whose name was to be Phillis, dropped anchor in Boston harbor, the Thirteen Colonies were becoming increasingly resentful of English domination. The soldiers of King George III patrolled the streets of Boston. When Phillis was in her early teens, in the street where she lived, a group of rebellious citizens clashed with the British soldiers. Among these angry Bostonians that night was a tall Negro seaman named Crispus Attucks. When the Red Coats fired, Crispus Attucks was the first man to fall, shedding his blood for American freedom. His body lay in state in Faneuil Hall, and today there is a monument to his memory in Boston Common.

Five years later the Revolutionary War began in earnest under the leadership of General George Washington. During the siege of Boston, Phillis wrote a poem about George Washington, terming him "first in peace." Its closing lines are:

> "Proceed, great chief, with virtue on thy side,
> Thy every action let the goddess guide.
> A crown, a mansion, and a throne that shine,
> With gold unfading, *Washington!* be thine."

From his encampment the man who was soon to become "The Father of His Country" wrote the young Negro poet a most gracious letter, thanking her for the poem—"however undeserving I may be of such encomium"—and paying tribute to her unusual poetic talent. He closed his letter by saying:

Phillis Wheatley

"If you should ever come to Cambridge or near headquarters, I shall be happy to see a person so favored by the Muses, and to whom Nature has been so liberal and beneficient in her dispensations.

I am with great respect,
Your Obedient Humble Servant,
George Washington."

When the Revolutionary War was over and our country had achieved its freedom, Phillis Wheatley composed one of her best poems, *Liberty and Peace,* which begins:

"Lo freedom comes. Th' prescient muse foretold
All eyes th' accomplish'd prophecy behold:
Her port describ'd, 'She moves divinely fair,
Olive and laurel bind her golden hair!' "

And its closing lines are:

Auspicious Heaven shall fill with fav'ring gales,
Where e'er Columbia spreads her swelling sails:
To every realm shall peace her charms display,
And heavenly freedom spread her golden ray."

New Englanders after the American Revolution continued to hold slaves, but the Wheatley family, perhaps in recognition of her genius, had already granted the young poet her personal freedom in 1772. Slavery for Phillis had not been harsh. She matured in a cultured home where, although it was most unusual for a slave to have a room alone, Phillis had her own room with heat and light so that she might read and write when her work was done. Certainly she profited by this generous consideration for the chronicles of her time report that she became one of the most cultivated young women in Boston—in a day when it was unusual for women of any race to be well read, to write poems, or to study Latin. Phillis read the Bible as well as Milton, Dryden, and other popular writers. Alexander Pope's translation of Homer was her favorite book, and his formal metres and carefully contrived couplets were the chief influence on her writing, in a day when the style in poetry was not personal, but high-flown and elegiac, with many references to classical gods and goddesses.

Famous American Negroes

This amazing young African poet was received in the homes of many friends of the Wheatleys. She became a member of Old South Church. Some of the leading personages of Boston were her patrons and her poetry was widely discussed. Some people claimed a slave could not possibly have written it, but others wrote letters to the papers saying that they knew for a fact that she did compose her own verses. Since she was not treated as a slave, in her poetry Phillis wrote of bondage hardly at all. But she had known in Boston slaves less fortunate than herself. And, in one passage in a poem dedicated to the Earl of Dartmouth, it is clear that she condemned slavery:

> "I, young in life, by seeming cruel fate
> Was snatch'd from Afric's fancy'd happy seat:
> What pangs excruciating must molest,
> What sorrows labour in my parent's breast?
> Steel'd was the soul and by no misery mov'd
> That from a father seiz'd his babe belov'd.
> Such, such my case. And can I then but pray
> Others may never feel tyrannic sway?"

Phillis was thirteen when she wrote her first verses. She was sixteen when she published, *On the Death of the Reverend George Whitfield*. And she was only twenty when, because of her frail health, her mistress permitted her to go on a sea voyage to England. It was in London that arrangements were made for the appearance of her first volume, *Poems on Various Subjects, Religious and Moral*. In England Phillis Wheatley was a guest of the Countess Huntingdon, who saw to it that she met many of the intellectuals there. The Countess was about to have her meet the King when, in Boston, Mrs. Wheatley became gravely ill, and Phillis sailed for home. Before she left, the Lord Mayor of London presented Phillis with a fine 1770 Glasgow folio edition of Milton's *Paradise Lost*.

Mrs. Wheatley did not live long after Phillis returned to Boston. And a few years later John Wheatley died. Their twins, Mary and Nathaniel, no longer lived in the family homestead for Mary was married and her brother was in Europe. Perhaps in search of a home and security, Phillis married a man, who, it turned out, was a jack-of-all-trades and a master of none,

Phillis Wheatley

This husband, John Peters, worked sometimes as a baker, sometimes a barber, sometimes a grocery clerk; and sometimes he sported a gold-headed cane and a powdered wig and said that he was a lawyer or a doctor. Maybe John Peters married Phillis because she was famous and he wanted, without too much effort on his part, to "be somebody." They had three children but he did not take care of them well. Two of them died in infancy. After the third child came, John Peters went away, leaving Phillis to work as a drudge in a poor boarding house. Both she and the baby fell ill and, in the cold of winter, at almost the same moment a little before Christmas, they died. They were buried together. The year was 1784. The first American edition of Phillis Wheatley's poems had just appeared in Boston.

In those days, as now, poetry brought in very little money. Phillis died in poverty. Following the funeral, her rare and beautiful edition of *Paradise Lost* was sold to pay the debts her husband had contracted. Now the book is preserved in the Library of Harvard University. Since her death there have been published at least eight editions of the poems of Phillis Wheatley. Today throughout America many schools, women's clubs, and branches of the Y.W.C.A. are named after this poet whose brief life encompassed Africa, Boston, London; the confines of slavery and the hospitality of royalty; fame and poverty; the poetry of Homer, Milton, Pope, and the drudgery of service in a boarding house. Towards the end of her life, Phillis Wheatley, perhaps out of shame and poverty, lost track of most of her friends. They were shocked and surprised to read in the papers a brief notice of her death.

But Phillis was never ungrateful for the good fortune that gave her early in life the kindly guidance of Susannah Wheatley. When Mrs. Wheatley passed away, Phillis wrote to a friend:

> "I have lately met with a great trial in the death of my mistress; let us imagine the loss of a parent, a sister or brother; the tenderness of all were united in her. I was a poor little outcast and a stranger when she took me in; not only into her house, but I was treated by her more like her child than her servant. No opportunity was left unimproved of giving me the best of advice; but in terms how tender! how engaging! This I hope ever to keep in remem-

brance. Her exemplary life was a greater monitor than all her pre-
cepts and instructions; thus we may observe of how much greater
force example is than instruction."

To a sensitive little African girl, under the circumstances of slavery, fate
could hardly have been more generous. The Wheatleys were good people.
But in spite of their kindness, as a child, sometimes in the night, Phillis
must have wept for her own mother. In the cold New England winters she
sometimes must have remembered the sunshine and the palm trees of far
away Senegal. In her teens as she read the measured rhythms of Pope by
candle light, dim in memory, perhaps the drums of Africa came to mind.
Did she try not to recall them because she knew she would never hear
them again? Did she maybe cry? Did she sometimes feel lost and lonely
like a motherless child? If she did, since it was not the fashion of her times
to be personal in poetry, she never wrote about it.

RICHARD ALLEN

RICHARD ALLEN

Founder of the African Methodist Episcopal Church

Born about 1760—Died 1831

RELIGION WAS A comfort that could not be denied even to a slave. In fact some slave owners used Christianity as an excuse for enslaving the African "heathen" in order, so they said, to save his soul. But once saved, they often made it difficult for him to worship God. Richard Allen, one of Negro America's first great ministers, was born a slave about 1760, in Philadelphia. He was sold while still a child to a planter in Delaware. As a young man he became a Methodist preacher and, with his master's permission, held religious services on the farm. His eloquence and sincerity were so great that he converted even his master. During the Revolutionary War Richard Allen earned money as a wagon driver and, by 1777, he had saved enough to purchase his freedom. He was twenty-six when he returned to Philadelphia to live as a free man.

Allen's gifts of pulpit oratory and mass leadership were such that many people were attracted to his prayer meetings. In those days there was no Methodist congregation in Philadelphia composed of Negroes, so young Richard joined the St. George Church, which some free and some slave colored people attended. At times he was even permitted to preach at St. George's. On such occasions Negro attendance at the church increased greatly —in fact, to such an extent that the officials suggested that colored worshippers be segregated. Some of the white members objected strongly to Allen's preaching, and some did not wish any Negroes in their church at all. One Sunday while Richard Allen and two friends, Absolom Jones and William White were bowed in prayer, they were rudely interrupted by an

11

usher, who literally snatched them from their knees and told them in no uncertain words that their presence was unwelcome. It was then that Allen, with the help of Jones, founded the Free African Society, a religious and civic organization that led to the formation of Bethel Methodist Episcopal Church, dedicated in Philadelphia in 1794 as a place where Negroes might worship in peace.

The year before this church was dedicated, a great epidemic of yellow fever spread with such rapidity throughout the city of Philadelphia that there were not enough doctors or nurses to attend the sick, and the dead were often left unburied. Since white people thought that Negroes did not seem to be dying of the disease in such great numbers as whites, and since many whites fled the city or were afraid to go near the ill or dead, a printed call was issued to the Negro citizens to attend the sick and bury the dead. Those who were slaves, of course, were forced to do this. But free Negroes were angered that such an unusual and dangerous request should be specifically directed to their race. A public meeting was called and Richard Allen and Absolom Jones, both being respected ministers, were appealed to for advice. After prayer and deep consultation, it was agreed that it was the duty of all Christians to help in the emergency as much as they could, so a committee of colored people called upon the mayor to offer their services to the city without reservation.

The Negroes of Philadelphia in large numbers went into white homes as nurses and aids. They tended the dying. They buried neglected corpses. A great physician of that day, Dr. Benjamin Rush, enlisted Allen and Jones as his special assistants. He quickly instructed them how to care for the disease and administer medicines, for many white doctors had died, others were exhausted, and some had taken their families—and themselves—away. There was panic in the city. No well person wanted to go near the sick, for fear of contagion. Without the ministration of the colored citizens, the dreaded plague might have decimated almost the entire population.

Nevertheless, when the siege was over, a white citizen, Mathew Carey, wrote *A Short Account of the Malignant Fever Lately Prevalent in Philadelphia* in which he praised Allen and Jones. But he asserted that on the

Richard Allen

whole the Negroes should have done much more, and also that some had profited financially by their labors. He singled out only the Negro citizens for such censure. Mathew Carey, it developed, had himself left the city at the height of the epidemic, while Allen, Jones, and most of the members of their churches had remained. During the plague some three hundred Negroes died. In answer to Mathew Carey, Allen and Jones wrote a reply, setting forth the true facts under the title, *A Narrative of the Proceeding of the Black People during the late Awful Calamity in Philadelphia*, in which they gave a listing of all monies received which, they said, had been less than enough to pay for the coffins bought and the labor hired. They related in detail their services, and stated how through religion they had "found the freedom to go forth, confiding in Him who can preserve in the midst of a burning furnace" for, they wrote, "The Lord was pleased to strengthen us, and remove all fear from us, and dispose our hearts to be as useful as possible." Certainly the Mayor and the City Council felt that the Negro citizens of Philadelphia had contributed greatly to the alleviation of the common distress during the terrible plague for they drew up a resolution formally thanking them for their services.

Richard Allen's fame as a minister and civic leader spread. And the Negro Methodists, under his leadership, rapidly grew in numbers. Mother Bethel, as his church was known, prospered. By 1820, there were over four thousand colored Methodists in Philadelphia. And churches of that faith under African Methodist Episcopal auspices had been established as far west as Pittsburgh and as far south as Charleston, South Carolina. But the great Denmark Vesey slave rebellion in Charleston in 1822 checked the spread of separate Negro churches in the South. The slave masters feared the unity which such congregations helped to develop among Negroes. Colored ministers were imprisoned and slaves whipped for going to church. And in Virginia, in 1830, after Nat Turner had led another slave uprising there, all Negro preachers were silenced by law. Nevertheless, Christians continued to hold meetings in woods, in cabins, and, sometimes when gatherings of any kind were strictly prohibited, a man or woman would worship alone where, as the spiritual says:

13

Wingate College Library

Famous American Negroes

"Way down yonder by myself,
I couldn't hear nobody pray."

Slave owners had good reason to fear the rise of a Negro church. They were beginning to realize that the old slave song they heard in the fields:

"Go down, Moses,
Way down in Egypt's land
And tell old Pharaoh
To let my people go. . . ."

was not just a song about the Israelites, but a cry of freedom born on the weary lips of enslaved men and women in their very midst. Out of the Negro churches then, and ever since, have come many distinguished leaders, ranging from Prince Hall who, about the time of the Boston Tea Party, established a church in Cambridge and became the founder of Freemasonry among Negroes, to Adam Powell, pastor of Abyssinia Baptist Church (the world's largest congregation of that faith) and a member of Congress from New York.

Richard Allen became a bishop of the church he had founded. But his activities extended far beyond his own faith. As the leader of the Free African Society he drew up many petitions calling for the abolition of slavery. He was a contributor to *Freedom's Journal*, America's first Negro newspaper. Under Allen's leadership three thousand Negroes met in Philadelphia in 1817 to register their opposition to the plans of the American Colonization Society to repatriate free colored peoples to Africa as a solution for the race problems of America. When some white proponents of colonization even went so far as to seize free men in the night and lash them until they were willing to say they wanted to go to Africa, out of self-protection the Negroes of New York, Pennsylvania, Delaware, and Maryland began to think in terms of a permanent organization to protect themselves from such indignities. The ever increasing enactment of laws "abridging the liberties and privileges of the Free People of Color" alarmed them, too.

In 1830 a committee which included Bishop Allen met in Philadelphia and constituted itself the first Colored Convention. Allen was elected president. It was agreed that the Convention would, "divise and pursue all legal means for the speedy elevation of ourselves and brethren to the scale and standing of men." The Negro people were urged by their leaders to be diligent, buy land, work to achieve unity, and to take advantage of "every opportunity placed within our power by the benevolent efforts of the friends of humanity in elevating our condition to the rank of freemen." It became obvious that these Negroes wanted full citizenship for themselves, freedom for their enslaved brethren, and a place as citizens in America where they were born, *not in Africa*. The constitution of this first Colored Convention was signed by Bishop Richard Allen.

Long before his death, Allen was recognized as one of the most distinguished citizens of the City of Brotherly Love. Today he is remembered chiefly as the founder of the African Methodist Episcopal Church. This denomination has well over a million members. It owns hundreds of beautiful churches, has established a number of accredited colleges, controls a great publishing house, and is a national force for good throughout America, and even abroad where its missionaries have gone as teachers and preachers.

IRA ALDRIDGE

Picture from Harvard Theatre Collection

IRA ALDRIDGE

A Star Who Never Came Home

Born 1807—Died 1867

THE FATHER of the first great Negro actor to be born in America was a minister, the Reverend Daniel Aldridge, pastor of a Presbyterian chapel in New York. When his son was born in 1807, the child was christened Ira. The records are not clear as to whether Ira Aldridge came into the world in Manhattan or somewhere in Maryland. But at an early age his name appeared on the rolls of the African Free School in New York City. And almost from that time on, his life is a matter of public record. He soon became an actor.

While yet in school, young Ira Aldridge carried a spear in mob scenes or filled in as a member of the crowd in performances at the African Grove on Bleecker Street. There in the early 1800's, a company of Negro actors presented Shakespearean plays and other dramas. The director, James Hewlett, starred in "Richard the Third" and "Othello." He also wrote a ballet in which he danced. The theater was not far from the Negro-owned Fraunces' Tavern where George Washington often dined. It was near the African Free School, too, which made it easy for young Ira to find his way there.

When white hoodlums began to make a practice of breaking up performances at the African Grove, the police forced the theater to close. The growing Ira Aldridge then took a job at night at the Chatham Theater where he could at least listen to the actors backstage. He took part in amateur theatricals, as well, and played one of the leading roles in Sheridan's play, "Pizarro." His love for the theater must have perturbed his father, a minister, for in those days playhouses were considered by the devout as dens of iniquity, and the

19

profession of acting did not rate highly. It might have been for this reason that the Reverend Aldridge decided to send his teen-age son abroad to further his education.

The University of Glasgow was known as being receptive to Negro students, and a number of anti-slavery leaders had been educated there. In Scotland Ira applied himself well to his studies, but it is not recorded that he remained long enough to graduate. He soon felt the lure of the stage again and, before he was twenty, he was playing the difficult role of Othello at the Royalty Theater in London. He was an immediate success. From that time on he toured the capitols of Europe regularly. Even in lands that did not understand his language there were long lines outside the theatres where he played. He was written about voluminously in the papers. His career spanned two generations. For forty years Ira Aldridge was a star.

At a theater in Dublin, the great English actor, Edmund Kean, saw Aldridge perform and was so taken with the power of his acting that he suggested they present "Othello" together, with Kean as the villian, Iago. Their production of this Shakespearean classic, which opened in London at Covent Garden in 1833, is reported to have been one of the greatest presentations ever. The two actors became close friends and for several seasons toured the English provinces and the Continent together. As the Moor in one of Shakespeare's most popular plays, Aldridge needed no makeup, being brown, tall, regal, and very handsome. His diction was clear, his voice resonant.

Although it was as Othello that Ira Aldridge received the greatest acclaim, he had mastered many other classical roles. He revived *Titus Andronicus*, which had not been staged in England for almost two centuries. In France the great Alexander Dumas, author of *The Count of Monte Cristo* and himself a man of color, was one of his admirers. The composer, Richard Wagner, was a follower of his performances. The King of Sweden issued a personal invitation to Aldridge to appear in Stockholm. The medal of the Order of Chevalier was conferred upon him by the King of Prussia, and the Czar of Russia granted him the Cross of Leopold. He was the sensation of Moscow and St. Petersburg during his performances there. Aldridge was often accorded the highest honor the students of Moscow University could bestow. They would

Ira Aldridge

unhitch the horses from his *droski* as he left the theater and themselves pull his carriage through the streets to the hotel.

An international star, Ira Aldridge had a long and colorful career as one of the greatest actors of his time. He was feted and lionized everywhere. After he became famous, he never returned to the land of his birth, but married and lived all his adult life in Europe. Still a star at the age of sixty, he died while on a tour of Poland. Today, in the Shakespeare Memorial Theater at Stratford-on-Avon, there is an Ira Aldridge Memorial Chair.

FREDERICK DOUGLASS

FREDERICK DOUGLASS

Fighter for Freedom

Born about 1817—Died 1895

Dᴜʀɪɴɢ ᴛʜᴇ ᴘᴇʀɪᴏᴅ when Ira Aldridge was playing Shakespeare, another American Negro became famous in Europe, too. He had crossed the ocean three times, once fleeing America for his life. But he did not remain abroad. He always came home to battle for the freedom of his people. His name was Frederick Douglass. His father was white but, nevertheless, Frederick was born a slave. His grandmother cared for him, and he never remembered seeing his mother more than a half dozen times in his life. The last time he saw her, she had walked twelve miles after dusk to hold him on her knees until he went to sleep. Then she had to walk twelve miles back to a distant plantation before sunrise to be at work in the fields.

When Frederick was born in the backwoods of Maryland, his name was not Douglass. It was Bailey. About the time when he was shedding his first teeth the boy was taken from his grandmother and, with a dozen other slave children, put into the care of a mean old hag on the plantation who whipped them often and frequently sent them to sleep on a dirt floor without their suppers. Frederick was ragged, neglected, and sometimes so hungry that he would wait at the kitchen door of the mansion house for the serving girls to shake the bones and crumbs from his master's table cloth. Then he would scramble with the dogs to pick up what fell into the yard. Fortunately, however, while still a young lad, he was sent to work for his master's relatives in Baltimore as errand boy and servant to that family's little son. Seeing that he was an apt boy, his new mistress taught him his A-B-C's. But her husband soon stopped her, saying, "If you teach him how to read, he'll want to know how to write, and this accomplished, he'll be running away with himself." However, white playmates in the streets sometimes lent him their bluebacked spellers and helped him to learn the words. When he was thirteen, with fifty cents earned from shining shoes, he bought a copy of *The Columbian Orator*, which included the speeches of William Pitt and other great men. This was his only book so he read it over and over. Many of the speeches were about liberty and freedom—as applied to white people, of course. But young Frederick took them to heart. "I wish myself a beast, a bird, anything rather than slave," he said.

His whole life eventually became a dedication to freedom. There was an old song he must have heard about "hard trials and deep tribulations." Such trials young Fred knew well. Meanwhile, he found comfort in religion under the guidance of a kindly old Negro named Lawson who could not read very well. Young Frederick taught Lawson "the letter" of the Bible; Lawson in turn taught Frederick "the spirit." Lawson strengthened his hope for freedom by assuring him, "If you want liberty, ask the Lord for it *in faith,* and He will give it to you." Frederick had begun to discover, too, that there were white people in America who did not believe in bondage. These were called *Abolitionists.* The Baltimore papers were always condemning them roundly as anarchists in league with the devil. But Frederick Douglass thought to himself that whatever the Abolitionists might be, they were not unfriendly to the slave, nor sympathetic to the slaveholder.

The more Frederick read the Bible and the newspapers, the more he began to realize that learning opened the way to achievement. As his master had warned, Frederick soon began to want to learn to write. In secret, at night in the loft where he slept, with a flour barrel for a table, his copy books being the Bible and a hymnal, the teen-age boy began to teach himself. When no one was at home, he sometimes borrowed his white master's pen and ink. In time he learned to write. When he was sent to work for another branch of the family in a small town, he found a Sunday school held there in the home of a free Negro. Frederick was asked to be one of the instructors. But on his second Sunday in this Sabbath school, a white mob rushed in armed with sticks and stones and drove everybody away. Young Fred was warned that if he kept on

Frederick Douglass

teaching Sunday school, he would be filled with shot. In the small community this sixteen-year-old slave who could read and write had gotten the reputation of being a "dangerous Negro," putting thoughts into other Negroes' heads. Shortly his apprehensive master sent him away to a "Negro breaker" to be made a better slave—that is, to be tamed, humbled, taught to be contented with slavery—in other words, "to be broken."

The man's name was Covey. His plantation was a sort of reformatory work-farm on a sandy, desolate point of Chesapeake Bay. Covey specialized in taking unruly young slaves for a year and "cutting them down to size," so that their masters would have no more trouble with them. Three days after Frederick arrived there, Covey gave him a team of untamed oxen and sent him to the woods for a load of logs. The boy had never driven oxen before, but he dared not object to the job. The oxen ran away, overturned the wagon, and smashed a gate. For this the sixteen year old lad had his clothes torn from him by the "slave-breaker," and was flogged on his bare skin with ox-goads. As he described it many years later in his autobiography, under Covey's "heavy blows blood flowed freely, and wales were left on my back as large as my little finger. The sores from this flogging continued for weeks, for they were kept open by the rough and coarse cloth which I wore for shirting . . . during the first six months I was there I was whipped, either with sticks or cow-skins, every week. Aching bones and a sore back were my constant companions." The scars which Covey put on Frederick's shoulders never went away.

Work from before dawn until long after sundown was a part of Covey's system. One day Frederick fainted in the broiling sun of the treading-yard where the wheat was being separated from the straws. He was dizzy. His head ached violently. He was deathly ill. When Covey commanded him to rise, he could not. The slaver gave him a series of savage kicks which finally brought him to his feet. Frederick fell down again, whereupon Covey took a hickory slab and struck him in the head, leaving him bleeding beside the fence. That night Frederick in despair dragged himself seven miles through the woods to his own master's house to beg that he be taken away from the slave-breaker.

But his master did no such thing. Instead, he accused the boy of trying to avoid work and sent him back the next day to finish out his year with Covey. Then it was that Frederick made up his mind to defend himself and never to let anyone mistreat him so again. He returned to the plantation but, it being the Lord's Day, Covey waited until Monday morning to flog him. To the slaver's surprise and chagrin, the tall young Negro had resolved to fight it out, man to man. Instead of submitting to a whipping, he flung the slave-breaker on the ground each time he came near. Covey finally gave up. Frederick was not whipped again as long as he was there. But Covey almost worked him to death.

"I was a changed being after that fight," Douglass wrote in his *Life And Times*. "I was *nothing* before; I was a *man* now." On Christmas Day, 1834, his year with the slave-breaker was up. But his spirit, far from being broken, had been strengthened. His hatred of the cruelties of slavery intensified. And his determination to be free grew ever stronger. When the boy was transferred to a new master, even though conditions were much more pleasant, he began to plan a break for freedom. Frederick persuaded five other slaves to run away with him. On the eve of their departure, someone betrayed them. Frederick was bound and dragged off to jail. When he was released, he was not wanted on that plantation any more. (He was a "dangerous Negro.") So he was sent back to Baltimore and put to work in a shipyard where he learned the calker's trade. But the white workers objected to Negroes working with them. One day a number of them ganged up on Frederick (who was certainly there through no fault of his own) and beat him almost to death. In fact, he was beaten so badly that his master, for fear of losing a valuable slave, did not send him back to the shipyards again. Instead, he allowed Frederick to hire himself out, providing that every Saturday night he turned *all* his wages in to his master. Sometimes he might let Frederick keep a quarter for himself. Eventually, Frederick managed to save enough secretly to pay his fare to New York. Though it might mean his life if he were captured, Frederick decided to dare to try to escape from slavery again. Disguised as a sailor, and with borrowed seaman's papers, he leaped on a train just as it was leaving Baltimore. A day later, he reached New York. He was twenty-one years old

Frederick Douglass

when he set foot on free soil. A dream had at last come true. *He belonged to himself.*

A new world had opened for him. "I felt as one might feel upon escape from a den of hungry lions," he wrote in his first letter to a friend. But soon his money was gone. In the big city nobody paid any attention to him. He was afraid to approach anyone, since he did not know whom to trust for fear he might be returned to slave territory. As he later described his condition, "I was without home, without acquaintance, without money, without credit, without work, and without any definite knowledge as to what course to take or where to look for succor. In such an extremity, a man has something beside his new-born freedom of which to think. While wandering about the streets of New York, and lodging at least one night among the barrels on one of the wharves, I was indeed free—free from slavery—but free from food and shelter as well."

A sailor who lived near the docks took him in, gave him a place to sleep, and put him in touch with a committee whose work it was to help escaped slaves. While in hiding in New York, Frederick was married to a girl with whom he had fallen in love in Baltimore and who followed him to the big city. Together they set out for Massachusetts on the deck of a steamer, for Negro passengers were not allowed in the cabins. In New Bedford he found employment on the wharves. There he dropped his slave name, Bailey, and took the name of one of the characters in *The Lady of the Lake*—Douglass. From then on he was known as Frederick Douglass, a name shortly to be in headlines around the world. For the young freeman was not satisfied just to be free himself. He became an Abolitionist.

In 1841, Douglass made his first talk at an Anti-Slavery Society meeting in Nantucket. There, groping for words, since he had never faced an audience before, he told the story of his childhood, his bondage, and his escape. People were deeply moved. William Lloyd Garrison, who followed Douglass as a speaker, cried, "Is he a man or a thing?" And proceeded to point out how, in spite of slave-owners treating Frederick as a *thing*, free people could see that here was a man, worthy of being treated as a man.

Douglass was then twenty-four years old, six feet tall, with hair like a lion, and very handsome. The more speeches he made, the more effective he became. Soon he was persuaded to quit his work on the docks and become an orator for the cause of freedom. In 1845 he made his first trip to England to tell sympathizers there about the plight of America's slave millions. When he returned he began to publish a paper in Rochester, called *The North Star*. From then on, for fifty years, Douglass was a great public figure. He spoke on platforms with many of the distinguished men and women of his times— Wendell Phillips, Harriet Beacher Stowe, Charles Sumner, and Lucretia Mott. He published his life story. He defied the Fugitive Slave Law of 1850 and sheltered runaways in his home. Mobs attacked his meetings. He was sometimes stoned. After John Brown's famous raid on Harper's Ferry, in which he had no part, the newspapers and the slave owners sought to implicate him. Douglass had to flee for his life to Canada, whence he made his second trip to England. When the War between the States broke out, he was back in this country, counselling with President Lincoln and recruiting troops for the Union Army—in which his own sons served. More than two hundred thousand Negroes fought in this War for freedom and the preservation of the Union. Many were inspired to do so by the brilliant speeches of Frederick Douglass.

When the War was over, Douglass became one of the leaders of the Republican Party. He was made a United States Marshall. Later he was appointed the Recorder of Deeds for the District of Columbia. And in 1889 he was confirmed as United States Minister to the Republic of Haiti. Active not just as a leader of the Negro people, at the first convention for women's suffrage Douglass was the *only* man of any color to stand up on the floor and defend the right of women to the ballot equally with men. "Right is of no sex," he stated in the first issue of *The North Star*. He was active, too, in the national temperance organizations and many other movements for social betterment. After Emancipation, Douglass demanded no special privileges for Negroes. For them he wanted simply the same freedom of action he felt *every* citizen should have. In a famous speech called, *What the Black Man Wants*, he said, "The American people have always been anxious to know what to do with us. I have had but one answer from the beginning. Do nothing with us! . . . If the Negro cannot stand on his own legs, let him fall. All I ask is, give him a *chance* to stand on his own legs! Let him alone! If you see him on his way to school, let him alone—don't disturb him. If you see him going to the dinner table at a hotel, let him go! If you see him going to the ballot box, let him alone—don't disturb him! If you see him going into a workshop, just let him alone."

The only school from which Douglass was ever graduated, as he often repeated, was the school of slavery. His diploma was the scars upon his back. But he had about him a wit and wisdom that many a better educated person did not possess. His speeches moved thousands to action. As a writer he left behind him his *Life and Times*, an autobiography that is an American classic. His simple but effective use of words, tinged sometimes with wry humor, is illustrated in the final paragraph of a letter he wrote to his former master on the tenth anniversary of his escape to freedom. In this letter he listed all the wrongs this man had done him, but closed by stating:

> "There is no roof under which you would be more safe than mine, and there is nothing in my house which you might need for your comfort, which I would not readily grant. Indeed, I should esteem it a privilege to set you an example as to how mankind ought to treat each other.
>
> "I am your fellow man, but not your slave,
>
> Frederick Douglass."

HARRIET TUBMAN

HARRIET TUBMAN

The Moses of Her People

Born about 1823—Died 1913

"THEN WE SAW the lightning, and that was the guns; and then we heard the thunder, and that was the big guns; and then we heard the rain falling, and that was the drops of blood falling; and when we came to get in the crops, it was dead men that we reaped." So the escaped slave, Harriet Tubman, described one of the battles of the War between the North and South in which she took part, for she was in the thick of the fighting. Before the War, like Frederick Douglass, Harriet Tubman devoted her life to the cause of freedom, and after the War to the advancement of her people.

Like Douglass she was born in Maryland a slave, one of eleven sons and daughters. No one kept a record of her birth, so the exact year is not known. But she lived so long and so much was written about her that most of the other facts of her life are accurately recorded. She was a homely child, morose, wilful, wild, and constantly in rebellion against slavery. Unlike Phillis Wheatley or Douglass, Harriet had no teaching of any sort, except the whip. As a little girl, on the very first day that she was sent to work in the Big House, her mistress whipped her four times. Once she ran away and hid in a pig sty for five days, eating the scraps thrown to the pigs. "There were good masters and mistresses, so I've heard tell," she once said, "but I didn't happen to come across any of them."

Harriet never liked to work as a servant in the house, so perhaps because of her rebellious nature, she was soon ordered to the fields. One day when she was in her early teens something happened that affected her whole life. It was evening and a young slave had, without permission, gone to a country

35

store. The overseer followed him to whip him. He ordered Harriet to help tie him up. As Harriet refused, the slave ran. The overseer picked up a heavy iron weight from the scales and threw it. But he did not hit the fellow. He struck Harriet's head, almost crushing her skull, and leaving a deep scar forever. Unconscious, the girl lingered between life and death for days. When at last she was able to work again, Harriet still suffered fits of unconsciousness. These lasted all her life. They would come upon her at any time, any place, and it would seem as if she had suddenly fallen asleep. Sometimes in the fields, sometimes leaning against a fence, sometimes in church, she would "go to sleep" and no one could wake her until the seizure had passed. When she was awake, this did not affect her thinking. But her master thought the blow had made her half-witted. Harriet continued to let him believe this. Meanwhile, she prayed God to deliver her from bondage.

When she was about twenty-four years old, she married a jolly, carefree fellow named Tubman, who did not share her concern for leaving the slave country. A few years later, when her old master died, Harriet heard that she and two of her brothers were to be sold, so they decided to run away, together. It was dangerous to tell anyone. Harriet had no chance to let even her mother know directly. But on the evening that she was leaving, she went about the fields and the slaves quarters singing:

"When that old chariot comes
I'm gwine to leave you.
I'm bound for the Promised Land. . . ."

And the way she sang that song let her friends and kinfolks know that to Harriet the Promised Land right then meant the North, not heaven. That night she left the Brodas Plantation on the Big Buckwater River never to return. Before dawn her brothers became frightened and went back to the slave huts before their absence was discovered. But Harriet went on alone through the woods by night, hiding by day, having no map, unable to read or write, but trusting God, instinct, and the North star to guide her. By some miracle she eventually got to Philadelphia, found work there, and was never again a slave.

But Harriet could not be happy while all her family were slaves. She kept

Harriet Tubman

thinking about them. So, some months later, she went back to Maryland, hoping to persuade her husband to come North with her. He said he did not wish to go. She led others Northward, however, and, within two years of her own escape, she had secretly returned to the South three times to rescue two brothers, a sister and her children, and a dozen more slaves. The Fugitive Slave Law of 1850 now made it dangerous for runaways to stop anywhere in the United States, so Harriet led her followers to Canada where she spent a winter begging, cooking, and praying for them. Then she returned to Maryland to rescue nine more Negroes.

During the first years of her own freedom, Harriet spent most of her time showing others how to follow in her footsteps. Her fame as a fearless leader of "freedom bands" spread rapidly. Shortly large rewards were offered by the slaveholders for her capture. But she was never captured, and she never lost any of her followers to the slave catchers. One reason for this was that once a slave made up his mind to go with her and started out, Harriet did not permit any turning back. Perhaps her experience with her two brothers when she first ran away accounted for this insistence. Her method of preventing frightened or weak travelers on the freedom road from returning to slavery, and perhaps being whipped into betraying the others, was simple. Harriet Tubman carried a pistol. When anyone said he could not, or would not go on, Harriet pulled her gun from the folds of her dress and said, "You *will* go on—or you'll die." The strength or the courage to continue was always forthcoming when her faltering companions looked into the muzzle of Harriet's gun. Through swamp and thicket, rain and cold, they went on toward the North. Thus everyone who started out with Harriet Tubman lived to thank her for freedom.

Long before the War between the States came, so many slaves were escaping, and so many white people in the North were helping them, that the routes to freedom became known as the "Underground Railroad." Secret "stations" where escaping slaves might be hidden, warmed, and fed were established in homes, barns, and sometimes even churches along the way. The Quakers were especially helpful and active in this regard. And a strong Anti-Slavery Society supported such activities. Slave owners were losing thousands of dollars worth of slaves by escape every year. Harriet Tubman became known as a "conductor" on the Underground Railroad. She was not the only "conductor" but she was the most famous, and one of the most daring. Once she brought as many as twenty-five slaves in a single band to freedom.

Another time she had in her party of runaways a big strong slave worth $1500. His name was Josiah Bailey and the Maryland countryside was plastered with posters offering a reward for his capture. There were ads in the papers for his return. On the way through New York City a friend of freedom recognized Bailey from the description in the papers and said, "I'm glad to meet a man whose head is worth fifteen hundred dollars!" Josiah was so shocked at being recognized and so afraid that he would be captured that a mood of deep despair descended upon him and he would not speak the rest of the trip. When the train was carrying the runaways across the bridge at Buffalo into Canada, Bailey would not even look at the wonder of Niagara Falls. But when they got on free soil and he was finally safe, he burst into song, and nobody could stop him from singing. He cried that at last, thanks to God, he was in Heaven! Harriet Tubman said, "Well, you old fool, you! You might at least have looked at Niagara Falls on the way to Heaven."

Harriet had a great sense of humor. She enjoyed telling the story on herself of how, not being able to read, she once sat down and went to sleep on a park bench right under a sign offering a big reward for her capture. When she began to make speeches to raise money for the cause of freedom, she often told jokes, sang, and sometimes even danced. She might have been a great actress, people said, because without makeup she could hollow out her cheeks and wrinkle her brow to seem like a very old woman. She would make her body shrink and cause her legs to totter when she chose to so disguise herself. Once, making a trip to Maryland to rescue some relatives, she had to pass through a village where she was known. She bought two hens, tied them by their feet and hung them heads down around her neck, then went tottering along. Sure enough, a slave catcher came up the street who might, she thought, recognize her, tottering or not. So she unloosed the squalling chickens in the middle of the street and dived after them, purposely not catching them so she

Harriet Tubman

could run down the road in pursuit and out of the slave catcher's sight, while all the passers by laughed.

Sometimes, knowing that her band of fugitives was pursued by angry masters, she would get on a train headed South—because nobody would suspect that runaway slaves would be going South. Sometimes she would disguise the women in her party and herself as men. Babies would be given a sleeping medicine to keep them quiet and then wrapped up like bundles. Sometimes she would wade for hours up a stream to throw the hounds off scent. In the dark of night when there was no North star, she would feel the trunks of trees for the moss that grows on the northern side, and that would serve as a guide toward freedom. Often when all seemed hopeless—although she never told her followers she had such feelings—Harriet would pray. One of her favorite prayers was, "Lord, you've been with me through six troubles. Be with me in the seventh." Some people thought that Harriet Tubman led a charmed life because, within twelve years, she made nineteen dangerous trips into the South rescuing slaves. She herself said, "I never run my train off the track, and I never lost a passenger."

Her father and mother were both over seventy years of age when she rescued them and brought her parents North to a home she had begun to buy in Auburn, New York. At first they stayed in St. Catharines, Canada, where escaped slaves were safe, since, in 1833, Queen Victoria had declared all slavery illegal. But it was too cold for the old folks there. And Harriet's work was not on foreign soil. She herself seemed to have no fear of being captured. She came and went about the United States as she chose. And became so famous that, although she never sought the spotlight, it was hard for her not to be recognized wherever she was. Once at a great woman's suffrage meeting where her old head wound had caused her to go sound asleep in the audience, she was recognized, and awoke to find herself on the platform. Her speech for women's rights was roundly applauded. In those days neither Negroes nor women could vote. Harriet believed both should, so, like Frederick Douglass, she followed the woman's suffrage movement closely.

In appearance "a more ordinary specimen of humanity could hardly be found," but there was no one with a greater capacity for leadership than she had. Among the slaves, where she walked in secret, Harriet began to be known as Moses. And at the great public meetings of the North, as the Negro historian William Wells Brown wrote in 1854, "all who frequented anti-slavery conventions, lectures, picnics, and fairs, could not fail to have seen a black woman of medium size, upper front teeth gone, smiling countenance, attired in coarse but neat apparel, with an old-fashioned reticule or bag suspended by her side, who, on taking her seat, would at once drop off into a sound sleep. . . . No fugitive was ever captured who had Moses for a leader." She was very independent. Between rescue trips or speeches, she would work as a cook or a scrubwoman. She might borrow, but she never begged money for herself. All contributions went toward the cause of freedom in one way or another, as did most of what she earned.

But when the War between the States began and she became a nurse for the Union Armies, and then a military scout and an invaluable intelligence agent behind the Rebel lines, she was promised some compensation. Technically she was not a registered nurse, and being a woman, she could not be a soldier. Yet she carried a Union pass, traveled on government transports, did dangerous missions in Confederate territory, and gave advice to chiefs of staffs. But she never got paid for this, although she had been promised $1800 for certain assignments. To Harriet this made no difference until, after the War, she badly needed money to care for her aged parents. Petitions were sent to the War Department and to Congress to try to get the $1800 due her. But it was never granted.

Harriet Tubman's war activities were amazing. She served under General Stevens at Beaufort, South Carolina. She was sent to Florida to nurse those ill of dysentery, small pox, and yellow fever. She was with Colonel Robert Gould Shaw at Fort Wagner. She organized a group of nine Negro scouts and river pilots and, with Colonel Montgomery, led a Union raiding contingent of three gunboats and about 150 Negro troops up the Combahee River. As reported by the Boston *Commonwealth*, for July 10, 1863, they "under the guidance of a black woman, dashed into the enemy's country, struck a bold and effective blow, destroying millions of dollars worth of commissary stores, cotton and lordly dwellings, and striking terror into the heart of rebeldom,

Harriet Tubman

brought off near 800 slaves and thousands of dollars worth of property." Concerning Harriet Tubman, it continued, "Many and many times she has penetrated the enemy's lines and discovered their situation and condition, and escaped without injury, but not without extreme hazard."

One of the songs Harriet sang during the War was:

"Of all the whole creation in the East or in the West,
The glorious Yankee nation is the greatest and the best.
Come along! Come along! Don't be alarmed,
Uncle Sam is rich enough to give you all a farm."

But Harriet Tubman never had a farm of her own. Her generous nature caused her to give away almost all the money she ever got her hands on. There were always fugitives, or relatives, or causes, or friends in need. She was over forty years old when Abraham Lincoln signed the Emancipation Proclamation, making legal for all the freedom she had struggled to secure. She lived for almost fifty years after the War was over. Some people thought she was a hundred years old when she died in 1913. Certainly she was over ninety.

A number of books have been written about her. The first one, *Scenes in the Life of Harriet Tubman*, by Sarah H. Bradford, appeared in 1869, and the proceeds from its sale helped Harriet pay for her cottage. She wrote her friend, Frederick Douglass, who had hidden her and her runaway slaves more than once in his home in Rochester, for a letter about her book. In his reply he compared their two careers:

"The difference between us is very marked. Most that I have done and suffered in the service of our cause has been in public, and I have received much encouragement at every step of the way. You, on the other hand, have labored in a private way. I have wrought in the day—you in the night. I have had the applause of the crowd and the satisfaction that comes of being approved by the multitude, while the most that you have done has been witnessed by a few trembling, scared and footsore bondsmen and women, whom you have led out of the house of bondage, and whose heartfelt, *God bless you*, has been your only reward. The midnight sky and the silent stars have been the witnesses of your devotion to freedom and of your heroism."

When years later, in her old age, a reporter for *The New York Herald Tribune* came to interview her one afternoon at her home in Auburn, he wrote that, as he was leaving, Harriet looked toward an orchard nearby and said, "Do you like apples?"

On being assured that the young man liked them, she asked, "Did you ever plant any apples?"

The writer confessed that he had not.

"No," said the old woman, "but somebody else planted them. I liked apples when I was young. And I said, 'Some day I'll plant apples myself for other young folks to eat.' And I guess I did."

Her apples were the apples of freedom. Harriet Tubman lived to see the harvest. Her home in Auburn, New York, is preserved as a memorial to her planting.

BOOKER T. WASHINGTON

BOOKER T. WASHINGTON

Founder of Tuskegee

Born about 1858—Died 1915

Booker T. Washington was a speaker at the memorial ceremonies for Harriet Tubman in Auburn, New York, the year after her death. He, too, had been born in slavery, but freedom came while he was still young, so Booker T. did not undergo the years of cruelty that Frederick Douglass and Harriet Tubman suffered. His struggle was to center in education, not freedom. And he was to become a teacher.

Like Frederick Douglass, Booker T. Washington's father was white, his mother a Negro slave, the plantation cook, and the cabin in which he was born was the plantation cookhouse. It had a dirt floor and no windows. With the fireplace constantly going, it was very hot in summer and very smokey in winter. There was a cat-hole in one wall, so the cat could come in and out at night. And, in the middle of the cabin, there was a plank-covered hole in the earth where sweet potatoes were stored. As a child the boy had only one name, Booker. It never occurred to him that he needed another name until he started to school after the War between the States.

During the War his step-father followed the Union armies. When, at the end of the War, all the slaves were freed, the man sent for his family to join him where he had found work in the salt mines at Malden, West Virginia. Booker was about eight years old when he, with the other slaves, stood in the yard before the porch of the "big house," where his master's family had gathered, and heard the Emancipation Proclamation read. Then the slaves were told that they were free. He heard their wild shouts of rejoicing and saw their happy tears. But the rejoicing lasted only a few days for, as Booker

45

wrote afterwards in his life story, *Up From Slavery*, "The great responsibility of being free, of having charge of themselves, of having to think and plan for themselves and their children, seemed to take possession of them. . . . In a few hours the great questions with which the Anglo-Saxon race had been grappling for centuries had been thrown upon these people to be solved. These were the questions of a home, a living, the rearing of children, education, citizenship, and the establishment and support of churches." They had no money, they had no land, they had nothing—but freedom.

In West Virginia little Booker was put to work at a salt furnace where his day began at four o'clock in the morning. At night he and his mother struggled together to learn the alphabet from an old speller she had somehow gotten for him. They had to learn alone because there was no literate person around who could help them. Then one day a young man who could read came to town, and all the colored people pooled their money and paid him to open a school for them. His pupils were of all ages, for every Negro wanted to learn. The older people wanted, at least, to be able to read the Bible before they died. For those who worked, the teacher held night classes. And folks who could get help at no other time, even took their spellers to Sunday school with them. Day-school, night-school, and Sunday school were all crowded. But the greatest disappointment of little Booker's life was that his step-father would not let him go to school. His family needed the money that he earned working all day at the salt furnace. Finally, with his mother's help, a few lessons at night were arranged. Then, at last, his step-father relented and said that if Booker would work from dawn until school time, and then go back to work after classes, he could go to day school when the new term started.

This is what happened on his first day at school. The teacher began by asking each pupil his name so that he could record it on the roll. As he went from row to row, Booker's heart began to thump madly, because every child there had two and sometimes even three names—but he had only one! He grew hot with shame and hung his head, puzzled, because he did not know what to do. Then, suddenly his turn came and he shouted out, "Booker Washington." He never knew how that second name happened to come into his head on the spur of the moment. But it did, so he kept it. Later he added a middle name, Taliaferro. But this was a hard name to pronounce and to spell, so from his youth on, his middle name served mostly to provide him with an initial. People always called him Booker T.

Since he was getting big enough now to work in the salt mines rather than just at the furnace, and his family needed all the money he could earn, he did not remain in school long. And from the salt mines, he went to the coal mines, deep underground, where the labor was not only hard, but dangerous. In the coal mines there was always the chance of being blown to pieces by an explosion, or crushed to death by falling slate. Sometimes Booker's light would go out and he would get lost in the enormous darkness. But it was in the coal mines that the boy first heard men talking about a school called Hampton in Virginia where, they said, one could work for an education. Young Booker T. decided to go there. Gradually he managed to save a little money. The old people in the community, proud of his determination to go away to school, gave him nickles, dimes, quarters, or the gift of a handkerchief or a pair of socks. From somewhere he got a battered old suitcase. Booker T. was fifteen years old. Hampton was five hundred miles away. One day he started out over the mountains in an old-fashioned stage-coach intending to ride as long as his funds lasted.

Late in the evening the stage-coach stopped at a ramshackle inn where the passengers were to take supper and be accommodated for the night. The travellers were all white except Booker T. When he presented himself at the desk, the proprietor rudely turned the Negro lad away, refusing to allow him food, or even to remain inside the building. All night the cold, hungry boy walked up and down the road to keep warm until the stage-coach started off in the morning. "This was my first experience in finding out what the color of my skin meant," he wrote in *Up From Slavery*, but, "My whole soul was so bent upon reaching Hampton that I did not have time to cherish any bitterness toward the hotel-keeper."

By the time Booker T. got to Richmond, all his money was gone, so he slept that night under a wooden sidewalk. When passing footsteps overhead woke him up in the morning, he found himself near the river where a vessel was unloading pig iron. The captain gave him work helping to unload the ship, so he remained in Richmond several days. But in order to save for the remainder of his trip, he continued to sleep under the sidewalk. As soon as he had a little money, he went on to Hampton, walking part of the way. He arrived there with exactly fifty cents to commence his education. As he entered the grounds and looked up at a big three-story building, it seemed to him the largest and most beautiful building he had ever seen, and he thought he was in paradise. But the picture changed when he presented himself, covered with the dust of the road, hungry, and tired, to Miss Mary F. Mackie, the head teacher. She thought he was perhaps a tramp and she had very grave doubts about admitting him. Since she did not definitely say, "No," however, he lingered in her office, becoming more and more discouraged as he saw other students being assigned to classes. Finally Miss Mackie said, "The adjoining recitation room needs sweeping. Take the broom and sweep it."

Young Booker T. knew that that was his entrance examination. He not only swept the room once, he swept it three times, moving all the furniture. Then he dusted it four times, putting everything carefully back in place. When he was through, he reported to the head teacher. She took her clean white hand-kerchief and rubbed it over the woodwork and the furniture, but she could not find a particle of dirt or dust. She looked at the anxious young Negro and said quietly, "I guess you will do to enter this institution." Miss Mackie gave him a job as a janitor and, by working late into the night cleaning the school rooms and getting up early in the morning to build the fires, Booker T. got his education and acquired the trade of bricklayer. He learned to read well, to speak clearly, to bathe every day, and to sleep *between* sheets. He was put into a dormitory room with seven other young men. He did not want them to know that he had never slept in a bed with sheets before, and that he did not know what to do with them. The first night Booker T. slept under both sheets. The second night he slept on top of both of them—until finally he found out that he should sleep *between* them. In 1875 he was graduated with honors from Hampton.

General Armstrong, the founder of Hampton Institute, and all the other white teachers there who had come into the South to help the freed Negroes gain an education, made a great impression on young Booker T. through their hard work, self sacrifice, sympathy, and understanding of the problems of their students, many of whom were older than the teachers. A conscientious New Englander, Miss Mackie herself, when not teaching, cleaned halls and washed windows along with Booker T., who wrote of such teachers years later, "What a rare set of human beings they were! They worked for the students night and day, in season and out of season. . . . Whenever it is written —and I hope it will be—the part that the Yankee teachers played in the education of the Negroes immediately after the War will make one of the most thrilling parts of the history of this country."

When General Armstrong, finding the school over-crowded and not wishing to turn away any new students, put up tents and asked for volunteers willing to sleep in them all winter, almost all the students volunteered, so great was their love for him. Booker T. was one who slept through the bitter cold that year in a tent that sometimes blew away in the night. But every morning the General would come to visit the young men in their tents and "his cheerful, encouraging voice would dispel any feeling of discouragement." Booker T. wanted to be like General Armstrong. So he became a teacher of the lowly, too.

After graduation he went back home to Malden to teach from eight o'clock in the morning until sometimes ten o'clock at night. The young man who had taught him had gone, so Booker T. was the only teacher. His night classes were as large as the day classes, for many working people wanted to learn. On Sundays he conducted two Sunday schools, one in town and one in the country. Meanwhile, he began to give private lessons to several young men that he was preparing to go, as he had done, to Hampton. Booker T. particularly wanted his older brother, who had, up to now, worked hard in the mines, to get an education. So he helped him learn to read and encouraged him to go to Hampton also. In fact, the students that Booker T. sent to Hampton from Malden made such a good record that General Armstrong was convinced they had had a good teacher. This caused him to invite Booker T. to return to Hampton to teach there and to supervise a dormitory for a hundred Indians coming to study. Booker T. and the Indians got along fine together. The Negro students cordially welcomed the "red men," took them as room-mates, and helped them to learn English. For a number of years Hampton was America's leading institution for both Negro and Indian students. Young Booker T. was "house father" to the Indians.

But in 1881 he was called deep into the Black Belt of the South to establish a school at Tuskegee, Alabama. A Negro shoemaker and a white banker had written General Armstrong to send them someone for that job. Armstrong sent Booker T. Washington. In a tumble-down old church with thirty students ranging in age from fifteen to forty, with himself as the only teacher, Tuskegee Institute, began. With no equipment, but with "hundreds of hungry, earnest souls who wanted to secure knowledge," Booker T. set to work. At first there were so many holes in the roof of his school that when it rained, one of the students held an umbrella over the teacher while others recited. The Alabama State Legislature voted $2,000 for teachers' salaries, but nothing for buildings or grounds. So Booker T. and his students decided to raise funds, buy land, and build a schoolhouse. They did. They planted the foundation and laid the bricks themselves. From a single room with a leaky roof to dozens of fine buildings, from one teacher to more than a hundred, from thirty students to three thousand, Tuskegee eventually grew until it became the most famous vocational school in the world, and Booker T. Washington gradually became America's most prominent Negro citizen.

The year after Booker T. opened his school, 255 Negroes were lynched in the South. The Ku Klux Klan had begun its terror. The use of the ballot, which an amendment to the Federal Constitution had granted the freedmen, was being taken away by state legislation. Prejudice and poverty, ignorance and despair, hung like a pall over the freedmen. What could a lone young teacher in the middle of Alabama do to help in such a situation? First the Negro people must be taught to work well, to keep clean, to be healthy, to be self-respecting, and they must learn how to better conditions right in their own houses, their own yards, and cultivate the soil where they were. That was one reason why Booker T. wanted his students to construct their own school buildings—so that they would learn how to build with their *own* hands and not be dependent on others. That is why he used part of the first land his school purchased for a farm. He soon acquired livestock and taught the students the care of animals. Behind all this was pride in working with the

Booker T. Washington

hands, in learning how "to do a common thing in an uncommon manner." He began by trying immediately to fit the school to the needs of the community—community of poor, unlettered, country people—and to prepare his students to "return to the plantation districts and show the people there how to put new energy and new ideas into farming, as well as into the intellectual and moral and religious life of the people." Tuskegee was the first institution to use farm and home demonstration methods, and to have a "movable school"—a truck carrying books and tools and teachers directly to the remote rural districts.

From the beginning Booker T. was able to get the help and advice of almost all the people of the countryside, both white and Negro. Even the poorest and oldest of the Negroes who had spent most of their days in slavery would bring gifts of coins, sugar cane, quilts, and cotton to Tuskegee. One day one old woman over seventy, and in rags, hobbled into the principal's office leaning on a cane with a basket on her arm. She said, "Mr. Washington, God knows I spent the best days of my life in slavery. God knows I's ignorant and poor. But I knows you is trying to make better men and better women for de colored race. I ain't got no money, but I want you to take dese six eggs what I's been savin' up, and I want you to put dese six eggs into de eddication of dese boys and gals." Later many large gifts came to Tuskegee from the wealthy and famous. Andrew Carnegie gave the school a lump sum of over a half million dollars. But no gift ever moved Booker T. Washington more than this old woman's gift of her six eggs.

With these people whom he taught and among whom he lived all his life, Booker T. never lost touch, even after he became internationally famous. President McKinley and his Cabinet visited Tuskegee. President Theodore Roosevelt invited Booker T. to luncheon at the White House. He was a guest of Queen Victoria at Windsor Castle when he visited England. But always when he came back to Tuskegee, whose principal he was until his death, Booker T. would join the farmers when they had a meeting on the campus, talk and joke and eat with them all day, and help them with their problems. Perhaps it was because Washington was as much at home in a black share-cropper's cabin as he was in a white Fifth Avenue mansion, that he became

51

a sort of liaison officer between the white people and the colored people of America. It was as a kind of statesman of the race problem that he grew to be better known even than he was as the educator of Tuskegee. The years of his adult life were some of the most difficult years for race relations in our country. The newly freed Negroes were determined to go forward. But there were some white Americans who were determined that they should not progress. There were white teachers willing to sacrifice their lives at schools for Negroes in the deep South. But there were also Klansmen who would burn down the schools and run the teachers away. The white hoods and robes of the Ku Klux Klan rode through the night terrorizing Negroes, and their white friends, as well.

Booker T. Washington sought a way to make peace between the races in the South. He said, "Any movement for the elevation of the Southern Negro, in order to be successful, must have to a certain extent the cooperation of the Southern whites." To that end, he made his famous speech at the opening of the Cotton States Exposition at Atlanta in 1895. Before an audience of thousands, Washington began by saying, "One third of the population of the South is of the Negro race." He then told his oft repeated story about a ship at sea signalling another ship for fresh water since it had none aboard. The other ship kept signalling back to cast down their buckets. Finally when the buckets were let down, the thirsty ship found that it was in a fresh water zone good for drinking. Washington continued, "To those of my race who . . . underestimate the importance of cultivating friendly relations with the Southern white man, who is their next-door neighbor, I would say, 'Cast down your bucket where you are.' Cast it down in making friends in every manly way of the people of all races by whom we are surrounded. Cast it down in agriculture, mechanics, in commerce, in domestic service, and in the professions. . . . No race can prosper until it learns that there is as much dignity in tilling the field as in writing a poem. . . . To those of the white race . . . I would repeat what I say to my own race, 'Cast down your bucket where you are.' Cast it down among the eight millions of Negroes . . . who have, without strikes and labor wars, tilled your fields, cleared your forests, builded your railroads and cities, and brought forth treasures from the bowels of the

Booker T. Washington

earth." Then came his most famous statement, "In all things that are purely social we can be as separate as the fingers, yet one as the hand in all things essential to mutual progress. There is no defense or security for any of us except in the highest intelligence and development of all."

For the next twenty years, from that time on until his death in 1915, Booker T. Washington was always consulted by civic leaders and politicians whenever any problems arose in regard to Negro citizens. He was considered *the* authority on Negro-white relations. And he was called upon to make hundreds of speeches all across the country. For years he was the center of a great controversy between those who agreed entirely with his Atlanta speech and its social program, and those who thought he did not stress strongly enough full equal rights for Negroes in every phase of American life. Because he believed in taking advantage of small opportunities, so some people felt, to the exclusion of greater ambitions, he was called an opportunist. Because he thought, so some people declared, that a half loaf was better than none, he was termed a compromiser. Because he did not protest color prejudice vigorously, but stressed rather making the best of things under the circumstances, some labeled him an "Uncle Tom." In later life he became a highly controversial figure.

But controversy did not lessen Booker T.'s fame. His school at Tuskegee grew until it became a little city in itself. On its founder were bestowed many honors. Harvard University awarded him the degree of Master of Arts, and Dartmouth College that of Doctor of Laws. His bust, designed by the distinguished Negro sculptor, Richmond Barthé, stands today in New York University's Hall of Fame. Booker T. Washington is buried on the campus at Tuskegee where boys and girls from the plantation country he loved still come to get an education. His letters and his speeches are in the Library of Congress. *Up From Slavery*, the story of his life, translated into many languages, is in the libraries of the world.

DANIEL HALE WILLIAMS

DANIEL HALE WILLIAMS

A Great Physician

Born 1858—Died 1931

Aʙᴏᴜᴛ ᴛʜᴇ ᴛɪᴍᴇ ᴛʜᴀᴛ Booker T. Washington was born in the South, another Negro boy destined to become famous was born in the North. At Hollidaysburg, Pennsylvania, in 1858, Daniel Hale Williams came into the world. His parents were free Negroes. His childhood was a happy one, spent with a brother and five sisters who did not know the trials and tribulations that slave children knew just a few miles farther South in Delaware and Maryland. Daniel went to school regularly and proved himself a bright pupil. But when, after his father's death, his mother moved with the other children to Janesville, Wisconsin, and Daniel was left with friends in Annapolis, he became lonesome for the rest of his family. One day he bundled up his clothes and went down to the railroad station and told the ticket agent how much he wanted to see his mother, but that he had no money to buy a ticket to Wisconsin. The ticket agent took pity on him and gave him a pass on the train. All alone, the boy, Daniel headed West.

His mother was so glad to see him that she did not scold him much for running away. But he had left all his school books behind and she did not have any money to buy him new ones. So, when he entered school in Janesville, all the ten-year-old boy had was an old dictionary. This he took to school with him every day and each strange word that came up in class, Daniel would look it up in his dictionary, underline it, and study it. Of course, he often found new words that he had never heard of at all. These, too, he would learn, so he soon had a very large vocabulary. He loved to read, and was particularly fascinated by history and the sciences. After grammar school, his mother encouraged him all the way through Hare's Classical Academy. But when he was graduated there, Daniel did not have the money to go to college, so he entered a law office in Janesville, thinking he would become a lawyer. But he did not enjoy the bitter quarrels and fights around which many law cases evolved, so he soon gave up that ambition.

His interest in the sciences caused him to begin thinking about being a doctor. But with such a large family, his mother could not help him any financially. Fortunately, a family friend, a barber named Mr. Anderson, took an interest in the boy and aided him in every way that he could. Soon young Daniel had the great good luck to be employed by the office of the Surgeon General of the State, Dr. Henry Palmer, where he could both work and study. From Dr. Palmer he learned a great deal about medicine, with the result that two years later he was able to pass the examinations and enter the medical school of Northwestern University, at Evanston, Illinois, where he remained until he was granted his M.D. degree. During the summers he earned his tuition by playing in an orchestra on the excursion boats on Lake Michigan. Because of his outstanding record as a student, Daniel Williams was asked when he was graduated in 1883, to remain on the campus at Northwestern as an instructor in anatomy. At that time it was most unusual for a large university to have a Negro instructor, so this appointment was indeed a real testimonial to his exceptional ability.

Young Dr. Williams began his professional practice as a surgeon at the Southside Dispensary in Chicago. Soon he became one of the doctors at the Protestant Orphan Asylum, too. Within a few years after he started his professional life in the great city on Lake Michigan, his services were so outstanding that he was invited to become a member of the Illinois State Board of Health. At that time, there were many young Negroes in Chicago who wanted to become doctors and Daniel Williams tried to help as many as he could. But none of the Chicago hospitals would accept them as interns, and there were no training schools where Negro women could study to become nurses. Only whites were admitted as nursing students. Dr. Williams decided to do something about this frustrating situation which he discussed at great length with other doctors and with city and state officials. As a result of his efforts,

Daniel Hale Williams

in 1891 Provident Hospital on the South Side of Chicago was established. In connection with it, the first Training School for Negro Nurses in the United States was opened.

While a surgeon at Provident Hospital, one day Dr. Williams performed an operation that was immediately heralded by newspapers and written about in medical journals around the world. It was the first time in history that such an operation had ever been done successfully. One day a man was brought into the emergency ward with a deep stab wound in the chest, bleeding profusely. Dr. Williams was called. He attended to the man. But the next day when he went to his bedside to see him, the man was worse, and still bleeding internally. To find out why this should be, Dr. Williams opened the wound and extended it so that he might discover the source of the trouble. He found that the man had literally been stabbed to the heart, and that there was a puncture in that vital organ. No one expected the man to live, but Dr. Williams decided to try to save him. The walls of the vessel surrounding the heart were cut and, while other doctors with forceps held these walls open, Dr. Williams carefully sewed up the knife wound in the man's heart. Then he replaced the walls of his heart while it continued beating. To do this required great skill, daring, and very steady nerves. The man lived. And the operation became a famous one in medical history.

The President of the United States, Grover Cleveland, invited the young Negro physician to come to see him in Washington. He offered him a position as head of the new Freedman's Hospital, recently established in the District of Columbia. Dr. Williams found in Washington the same needs for the training of student doctors and nurses of color as he had in Chicago. So he established in connection with Freedman's Hospital a nurses' training school. And during his five years there he made the hospital a welcome place for young Negro doctors to practice their internships. He was not only a distinguished surgeon, but a great organizer and administrator. He had many requests to head hospitals or to teach, but he returned to his own private practice in Chicago. However, once a year he held a demonstration clinic in surgery at Meharry Medical College in Nashville, attended by young doctors from many states who came to watch his operations.

In the early 1900's, Dr. Williams became a member of the surgical staff of Cook County Hospital in Illinois and later an associate surgeon at Chicago's famous St. Luke's Hospital. In 1913 he received the exceptional honor of being made a Fellow of the American College of Surgeons. He attended most of the leading medical conventions and clinics of our country for many years. When he died, Daniel Hale Williams had long been considered one of America's greatest physicians.

HENRY OSSAWA TANNER

HENRY OSSAWA TANNER

Whose Painting Hangs in the Luxembourg

Born 1859—Died 1937

Henry Ossawa Tanner did not leave behind him a dramatic life story, but he left many beautiful paintings in the museums of Europe and America. He wanted to be an artist and he became one. His father was a bishop of the African Methodist Episcopal Church so as a child, although his family was by no means rich, Henry did not know hunger or the darkness of ignorance. He was born in Pittsburgh, but early in life was taken to Philadelphia where he grew to young manhood. As a boy walking in Fairmont Park one day, he saw an artist painting a view of the park. Then and there he decided he wanted to be an artist.

Henry went home and immediately painted a picture on the back of an old geography, the same scene, as nearly as he could remember it, that the man was painting that afternoon. Soon, the youngster got some clay and began to make models of the animals in the Philadelphia zoo. Later he became impressed with some canvasses he saw of the sea, so he made a trip to Atlantic City during his teens especially to paint the ocean. All of this seemed very impractical to his father who thought that art was for vagabonds. Nevertheless, young Tanner enrolled at the Pennsylvania Academy of Fine Arts. And it was not long before he sold a painting for $40.00—a price which astonished him, for if he sold a picture for five or ten or fifteen dollars, he considered himself lucky. Even his very early paintings must have had some appeal, because one that he had sold for $15.00 was later resold at public auction for $250.00.

When young Tanner finished his studies at the Academy, he took a position as a teacher of drawing at Clark University in Atlanta. There, to supplement his meagre salary, he opened a photograhic studio. He continued painting in his spare time, too, and sold an oil entitled "A Lion At Home" for $80.00. The venerable Bishop Daniel A. Payne, a colleague of Henry's father and a friend of Frederick Douglass, became interested in his painting and gave him a great deal of help. Young Tanner made a bust of the Bishop, and the Bishop in turn acquired three of the youthful artist's pictures which he presented to Wilberforce University. In 1891 Tanner had enough paintings for a one-man show, so he organized an exhibition in Cincinnati. But there he did not sell a single picture. Again, however, a generous churchman, learning that the artist wished to go abroad, came to his rescue with the sum of about $300.00 so that Tanner might study in Rome.

On the way to Italy, Tanner stopped in Paris—and it was several years before he got any further! He was entranced, as artists have always been, with the art center of the world, so there he remained, studying first at the Academy Julien and later with various French masters of the era. Constant, Gerome, Jean Paul Laurens, and Thomas Eakins especially influenced his work. But it was the beauty and artistic freedom of Paris that really caused the young painter to turn out canvas after canvas. And in a few years, one of his oils had received honorable mention, his first official recognition, at the French Salon. Perhaps it was his close family connection with the church, and his childhood familiarity with the great Bible stories, that caused the budding artist to turn toward religious subjects. He traveled a great deal in the Holy Land, studying the people, the architecture, the shrines, and the relics there, and for a long period he confined his canvases almost entirely to Biblical subjects. In 1897 his "The Resurrection of Lazarus" was bought by the French government to hang in the Luxembourg, one of the world's great galleries. Crowds came to view it, critics praised it, and from that time on Tanner's reputation as a painter of merit was solidly established.

At the Paris Exposition of 1900 his work received a medal of honor. That same year he was awarded the Walter Lippincott Prize in Philadelphia, and shortly thereafter he brought a number of his paintings from Europe to the

Henry Ossawa Tanner

United States for an exhibition in the city where he had grown up. But Tanner did not remain in the land of his birth long. To his friends he confided that, as a Negro, he found life in Europe much less difficult, for there he could travel freely and without segregation. When he wanted to paint rural landscapes, he had no difficulty because of color in finding an inn at which to sleep, or a place to eat. So, like the actor, Ira Aldridge, before him, his career flowered in Europe. He resided abroad until his death in Paris. His beautiful studio attracted many visitors. Some of the great artists of the day were his friends. And he lived to see his paintings bring him a sizable income.

Tanner's fame rests chiefly on his contributions in the field of religious painting. His life-like figures of Biblical characters in dramatic poses, his use of light to symbolize the presence of God, his combination of mysticism and realism, had a wide popular appeal. Richly academic in style and visually naturalistic, his work was never difficult for the layman to understand, yet it possessed the technical excellencies and strength of craftsmanship that also brought him the approval of his fellow artists. Tanner's "Christ Walking on the Water," "The Disciples on the Road to Bethany," "The Flight into Egypt," and "The Miraculous Draft of Fishes" are moving portrayals of familiar scriptural scenes that people love. In Philadelphia's Memorial Hall in Fairmont Park today, not far from the spot where the idea of being an artist came to Tanner, his beautiful painting, "The Annunciation," hangs.

GEORGE WASHINGTON CARVER

GEORGE WASHINGTON CARVER

Agricultural Chemist

Born about 1864—Died 1943

ONE OF THE MOST important things that Booker T. Washington ever did was to engage George Washington Carver as a teacher at Tuskegee. Like Washington, Carver had been born in slavery. Shortly after his birth on a farm near Diamond Grove, Missouri, his father was run over by a wagon and killed. And before George was a year old, a band of Night Riders who made a specialty of kidnapping slaves and selling them to other masters far away, surrounded his mother's cabin in the night. An older brother escaped capture, but little George and his mother were tied on a horse and taken over the Ozark Mountains into Arkansas. No one knows what became of his mother. But their master, Moses Carver, sent a man looking for them. Having no money, the master offered the man a tract of land if he found the woman, and a horse if he found the child. The baby George contracted whooping cough, so the callous Night Riders abandoned him somewhere on the road, to continue their journey with the mother who was never seen again. But the man found the sick child and brought him back to his master, who gave the promised horse as a reward for the baby.

The Carver family kept little George, and gave him their name. They were kind people, with no other slaves and no children, so they reared the child and his brother almost as if they were their own sons. And, even though slavery had ended with the War between the States, the boys stayed with them. As a child, while his older brother was at work, little George had a great deal of time to roam the woods and the fields nearby. He was always bringing back to Mrs. Carver some strange root or plant that he had found,

69

wanting to know what it was. He seemed to have more than a normal child's curiosity about what made the petals of flowers different colors, why leaves had varying patterns, why bees loved clover, or why dew-drops sparkled. The Carvers were not educated people, but they answered his questions as best they could. And, noting his intelligence, they secured for him a spelling book which he and his brother puzzled over before the fireplace at night. But the days he spent mostly alone out of doors, often trying literally to get at the very roots of growing things, to puzzle out why the acorn made a tree, the sunflower seed a flower. He made himself a secret garden to bring back to life sick plants. He loved the feel of the earth in his little hands. Many years later he said, "People murder a child when they tell it to keep out of the dirt. In dirt is life."

George was about ten years old when his big brother decided to leave the farm to look for work elsewhere. Then the boy was more lonely than ever, except when he was busy helping the Carvers. Mrs. Carver taught George to cook and to clean and even to sew. He tended the fires in winter and learned to save the ashes to make soap. In Spring he cut sassafras bark and searched the woods for herbs and spices for medicines and seasonings. He helped spin flax and wool, tan cowhides for shoes, and boil barks for dye. By now he had learned every word in his old blue-backed speller. And he had heard that there was a school for colored children at Neosha, eight or ten miles away. He begged the Carvers to let him go there, and they did. He walked. A big strong kindly colored woman named Mariah Watkins took him in, and let him work for his board and keep. But she mothered him, too, and loved him, and his months with her became the happiest of all his young life. He was particularly happy because he could sit on a log bench in a log-cabin school with seventy other children and learn from their one teacher.

Being a washer woman, Mariah Watkins taught young George to wash and iron. For this he was in later years to be deeply grateful. Mariah Watkins gave him a Bible, too, that became his most cherished possession. For seventy years, no matter where he went, he kept that Bible. Because there was no high school in Neosha, when he was about thirteen George hitch-

George Washington Carver

hiked a ride in a covered wagon to Kansas. There, at Fort Scott, he entered high school, working meanwhile as a houseboy for the richest family in town. One evening his employers sent him downtown to the drugstore. Near the courthouse he observed a great crowd of white men milling about. And, as he stopped to watch, he saw them storm the jail, break down its doors, drag a poor helpless Negro into the street, and kick and beat him to death. Meanwhile other men and boys were building a bonfire in the town square and, when it was blazing high, they threw the bleeding Negro into it. Young Carver's heart almost stopped beating and he became sick at the stomach. That night the boy packed up his few belongings and left town.

For almost ten years he wandered about the western country, from place to place, town to town, harvesting wheat, cutting wood, working sometimes as a gardener, sometimes as a cook, sleeping on haystacks, in sheds, in stables. Whenever he could, he worked among plants and flowers. But having no garden of his own in which to grow flowers he began to draw and paint them as he saw them in other people's gardens. Once in a town called Minneapolis, Kansas, where he had stopped long enough to finish high school, a lady saw some of his paintings on the walls of her laundress' home. She admired them, and encouraged the young man to keep on painting. For, by now, he was a young man, tall and dark and thin and a little stooped from not having always had enough to eat and from working very hard. Being still curious about the flowers he painted, George wanted to study botany.

One day Carver saw in a newspaper an advertisement of a religious college at Olanthe, Kansas, called Highland University. He sent his high school record there and received a letter complimenting him on his good grades and saying that he would be registered. So, in the fall, he journeyed to that town, ready to study. But when he presented himself at the office to enroll, the minister in charge of the college looked at him in astonishment and said, "Why, we don't admit Negroes here!" He would not permit Carver to register. So the disappointed young man continued to wander across the western plains until he became a homesteader on some newly released government land. But he had no tools to develop the claim he had staked out, and no money to pay the taxes, so he lost the land. Although he was now more than twenty-five years old, George Washington Carver was still determined to complete his education. Finally, he gained admittance to Simpson College, near Winterset, Iowa. When he arrived there, so one of his teachers said later, he had only "a satchel full of poverty and a burning zeal to know everything."

Young Carver had but ten cents left after he had paid his entrance fees. With this he bought a nickel's worth of corn meal and a nickel's worth of beef suet which fed him for a week. Somehow he was able to persuade the general store to let him have two tin tubs, a washboard, some blueing, and some soap on credit. And he announced to the other students that he was opening a one-man laundry. That is how he earned his way through his first year of college, using the knowledge Mariah Watkins had taught him about washing and ironing. He had a beautiful high thin tenor voice and a talent for the piano and organ, so he studied music as well as the natural sciences. And, because he liked to paint, he studied art. Curiously enough, it was his painting that led to his further education. When his art teacher discovered his great interest in plants and soil, she wrote to her brother who was a professor of horticulture at Iowa State College at Ames, where there is an excellent agricultural department. Through this teacher Carver was admitted to classes there and became the first Negro to graduate from that institution.

But not all was smooth sailing at Iowa State where colored students were a rarity. Carver was not permitted to have a room in the dormitory. And, when he went into the student dining hall to eat, he was ordered out. But he was determined not to be discouraged, so he got a job as a waiter in the dining room and ate his meals free in the kitchen. Kind-hearted teachers or students often wanted to help him with gifts of old clothing or money, but he would never accept charity from anyone. He always insisted on working for everything that he received. His love of plants and painting combined caused him to win several prizes for his still-life canvases at the Iowa Exhibit of State Artists. And four of his pictures were sent to the World's Fair at Chicago. His graduation thesis was "Plants as Modified by Man." He stood at the top of his class in scholarship. And by the time he was grad-

George Washington Carver

uated in 1894, he had become so popular with his classmates that he was chosen the Class Poet. He ate his graduation dinner with his class in the very dining room that had at first turned him away.

George Washington Carver remained at Ames for two more years to do further study leading to an M.A. degree, and he was made an assistant instructor in Botany and put in charge of the greenhouse. Meanwhile, offers of jobs came to him from a number of Southern Negro colleges. One of his professors at Ames wrote in reply to such a request, "I do not want to lose Mr. Carver from our staff here. . . . In cross-fertilization and the propagation of plants he is by all means the ablest student we have. . . . With regard to plants he has a passion for them, in the conservatory, the garden, the orchard, and the farm. In that direction we have no one who is his equal." But, shortly after he had gained his second degree in 1896, Booker T. Washington came to the campus of Iowa State College and met George Washington Carver. He invited him to come to Tuskegee as head of the Department of Agriculture, director of agricultural research, and a teacher of natural sciences. A pretty heavy program, but, intrigued by the problems of this growing school in the Southland, Carver went, and remained there the rest of his life. It was at Tuskegee that he eventually became as famous as Booker T. Washington.

The two men were very different, and yet they had a great deal in common. Both had come up the hard way. Both believed in and loved working with the hands. Both had a deep feeling for the earth and all growing things. Both wanted to give what they learned to others. But George Washington Carver was a shy man and very quiet. Booker T. Washington was already a great public figure, a speaker able to sway large audiences, and an administrator accustomed to working with many people. Carver preferred to work alone, then present the results of his work to the world. The principal of Tuskegee understood this for he soon gave his new teacher a laboratory of his own, and a sleeping room of his own, and so Carver remained at Tuskegee the rest of his long life, living in one room and working in another. The Bible that Mariah Watkins gave him went with him to Tuskegee, too, resting on his bed table. His college textbooks went, also. But when

Carver worked in his laboratory he took no books of any sort into the lab. Every morning before sunrise he sat alone on a stump in the woods just behind his laboratory and talked with God. Then he went to work alone until the hour to meet his students. From Carver's small laboratory at Tuskegee came formulas in agricultural chemistry that enriched the entire Southland, indeed the whole of America and the world.

Tuskegee was situated in the Cotton Belt where everybody had been taught to raise cotton up to the very doorsteps. Cotton had taken all the richness out of the land. Besides, it was no longer as profitable as it had once been It was a risky crop. One of Tuskegee's problems was to teach the farmers to raise other things, and to save the land by rotating crops. In this Carver's help was inestimable. He showed them particularly the practical value of raising sweet potatoes and peanuts, and the variety of profitable products that could be obtained from these two plants. It was at Tuskegee that he began his famous experiments in finding out how many different kinds of useful things could be derived from the Alabama earth, particularly from the peanuts and sweet potatoes which grew so easily there. Before his death Carver had succeeded in extracting from the peanut such varied by-products as linoleum and metal polish, vegetable-milk and ink, grease, cooking oils, nineteen shades of dyes and stains, food sauces, shampoo, peanut butter, and cheese. Also, he evolved one hundred cooking recipes based on the peanut, from which a housewife could serve a full-course dinner—from soup to nuts!

In his little laboratory near the woods, Carver learned to create from sweet potatoes a valuable rubber compound, starch, imitation ginger, library paste, vinegar, shoe blacking, wood-filler, rope, flour, instant coffee, molasses, and almost a hundred other things. From pecans he produced many varied products. From cornstalks he taught his students how to make insulation wall-boards. Others of his products were synthetic marble from sawdust, plastics from wood-shavings, and writing paper from the wistaria vines that grew in profusion. From the Alabama clay itself, he showed that beautiful dyes of all colors could be made in quantities large enough to dye all the clothes in the world any shades people might desire. "Let down

George Washington Carver

your bucket where you are," became Carver's agricultural maxim. To take what one had and make it yield what one wished, became Carver's goal. Using the products of the land in the immediate vicinity of Tuskegee, he eventually benefited not just Alabama but people everywhere. Out of his experiments with the peanut grew a two hundred million dollar industry in the South. When he was called before a Senate Ways and Means Committee in Washington to explain what he had done with peanuts, the busy senators allotted him ten minutes. But once Carver had begun demonstrating peanut possibilities, they became so excited they let him talk for two hours. And, as a result of the information he gave them, they put through a tariff law to protect American peanuts from foreign competition.

Many universities awarded George Washington Carver honorary degrees, including that of Doctor of Science from the University of Rochester, so he became known as Dr. Carver. He was made a Fellow of the British Society of Arts, received the Spingarn Medal for outstanding achievement among Negroes, and many other honors. But he never enjoyed public life and could not often be persuaded to leave his laboratory to make a speech. President Franklin D. Roosevelt stopped at Tuskegee in 1939 to greet Dr. Carver. Henry Ford visited him there and they became great friends. But when Thomas A. Edison sent for Dr. Carver to work in his laboratories, offering him over fifty thousand dollars a year, he would not go. Neither would Carver ever apply for a patent on any of his discoveries. He said, "God gave them to me. Why should I claim to own them?" He cared nothing about money and would never accept a raise in salary at Tuskegee. Often, indeed, he did not even cash his salary checks. Once when asked for a contribution to some fund or other, he said that he had no money. Then he remembered to reach under a corner of his mattress. He pulled out a bundle of uncashed checks and said, "Here, take these. Maybe they are still good."

Although he had no interest in new clothes and never really dressed up, whenever Carver took off his laboratory apron and put on a jacket, he wore a fresh flower in his button hole. His speaking voice, like his singing voice, always remained high. Will Rogers once said of him that he was the only man he ever heard who could lecture to a class and sing tenor at the same time. All his life Carver continued to paint, and great museums sometimes tried to buy some of his paintings, but he usually would not sell any. Yet he would give them away, often to farmers or students. As he grew older some people thought he was a very strange old man. Everybody knew he was very famous. So, putting two and two together, they called him a genius. He was. "The wizard of the sweet potato" was a great agricultural chemist who did more in his field than any other single human being to advance the science of chemurgy—which means chemistry at work. When *The Progressive Farmer* once selected him as "the *Man of the Year* in service to southern agriculture" and all the nation's papers carried the news, *The New York Times* asked editorially, "What other man of our time has done so much for agriculture and the South?"

Ten years after his death, the United States government acquired the farm in Missouri on which George Washington Carver was born, and in 1953 it was dedicated by the Secretary of the Interior as a permanent shrine to his memory. On that occasion *The New York Herald Tribune* said:

> "It is fitting that there should be a national memorial to Dr. George Washington Carver. He rose from slavery to become a famous scientist. The list of his achievements as a benefactor of mankind is almost endless. . . . Dr. Carver, however, will be remembered in the gallery of great Americans not so much for scientific eminence, but rather for the quality of the man's spirit. He was, as every one knows, a Negro. But he triumphed over all obstacles, including that of racial discrimination. Perhaps there is no one in this century whose example has done more to promote a better understanding between the races. Such greatness partakes of the eternal. Dr. Carver did more than find hidden merits in the peanut and the sweet potato. He helped to enlarge the American spirit."

ROBERT S. ABBOTT

ROBERT S. ABBOTT

A Crusading Journalist

Born 1870—Died 1940

Robert Sengstacke Abbott was born on St. Simon's Island off the coast of Georgia in 1870, the son of a minister. He grew up in Savannah where he attended Beach Institute, and later Claflin Institute at Orangeburg, South Carolina. Then he went to Hampton where he was graduated as a printer. As a child he loved books and, fortunately, there was a good library in his home. He became acquainted with newspaper work early as an apprentice printer in the shop of the *Savannah News*. But since opportunities for advancement in printing were very limited for Negroes in the South, young Abbott settled in Chicago. There in 1896 he applied for membership in the Printer's Union, but was advised that he would only be wasting his time and money by belonging, since the union did not encourage colored membership. Nevertheless, he insisted on joining since all the big printing shops in Chicago were unionized. But, being a Negro, he found it very difficult to get work. And he learned that the union itself advised shops not to employ Negroes.

Frustrated in efforts to earn a living at his trade, he turned to the study of law at Kent College, and practiced for a while in Chicago and Gary. But he loved the smell of printer's ink, so he determined to start a newspaper of his own and eventually to buy a printing press. Besides, he felt that with all the problems Negroes had to face, they needed a mouthpiece in Chicago to air their grievances and to work for more democratic conditions in regard to employment, civil rights, and education. On the day that he began his paper he had only twenty-five cents, a desk, and a chair. A woman lent him a basement room on State Street which was at the same time her kitchen.

He solicited advertisements, gathered news, wrote editorials, printed, and sold the paper himself. The first issue of *The Chicago Defender*, dated May 5, 1905, consisted of three hundred copies. Its paper and printing cost $13.75. Three friends became subscribers at $1.00 a year. It was to appear weekly at five cents a copy. From the very beginning its issues grew in numbers of copies. Gradually the paper increased in size, too, and its subscribers became more numerous until they eventually numbered a quarter of a million and *The Chicago Defender* became the largest and most influential Negro newspaper in America.

As a boy in the deep South, Abbott had observed that almost the only news which the papers carried about Negro citizens was crime news or lynchings. When Negroes in Savannah died, or got married, or dedicated a new church, there was nothing in the daily press about these happenings. Many Southern papers made it a rule never to publish the picture of a Negro, not even Booker T. Washington's. And in writing about colored people, they usually refused to use the terms Mr. or Mrs. before their names. In the North, general news usually crowded the news of Negro activities out of the papers, unless again these were criminal activities. When colored boys and girls were graduated from high school or college, or won prizes, or gave a party, they liked to see their pictures in the paper, too. So, to supply the Negro community of Chicago with news of its own activities, as well as to provide editorial leadership in its struggle for democracy, Robert S. Abbott started *The Chicago Defender*. Gradually it grew into a national journal on sale on the newsstands of cities and towns almost everywhere. But, because of its strong stand on equal rights for all, various Southern communities refused to permit it to circulate. And, at one time in some counties in Georgia where Negroes could not vote, it was a crime—inciting to riot—for a colored person to possess a copy of this Northern newspaper with its accent on the ballot as the basis of democracy.

When Mr. Abbott began publishing the *Defender*, the Negro population of Chicago was about 40,000. But during World War I there was a great influx of colored people into the North, drawn by the war industries there, so by 1920 Chicago had over 100,000 Negro citizens. Because thousands of

Robert S. Abbott

men had gone off into the army, thus creating a labor shortage, factories and foundries that formerly had barred colored workers, now began to employ them, and the *Defender* urged that more do so. At that time Mr. Abbott wrote:

> "There is no line of endeavor that we cannot fit ourselves for. These same factories, mills and workshops that have been closed to us, through necessity are being opened to us. We are to be given a chance, not through choice but because it is expedient. Prejudice vanishes when the almighty dollar is on the wrong side of the balance sheet. . . . Slowly but surely all over this country we are gradually edging in first this and then that place, getting a foothold before making a place for our brother. By this only can the so-called race problem be solved. It is merely a question of a better and a closer understanding between the races. We are Americans and *must* live together, so why not live in peace?"

A firm believer in the power of the ballot, *The Chicago Defender* urged Negroes to register, vote, and elect their own representatives to office. Shortly there were colored aldermen in the City Council of Chicago, Negro representatives in the Illinois State Legislature, and Oscar DePriest was elected the first Negro to serve in Congress at Washington since the turn of the century. In these political gains Editor Abbott's paper played no small part. While urging Negroes to take advantage of their democratic rights, it at the same time continually urged them to shoulder their full civic and national duties, to keep their neighborhoods clean, be thrifty and self-respecting, buy bonds, aid the war effort, and in general be good citizens.

Because, until very recently, the big national advertisers like the makers of motor cars and breakfast foods, did not advertise in Negro newspapers, these papers had to depend almost entirely on newsstand sales and subscriptions for income. Realizing this, Mr. Abbott instituted colorful and dramatic reporting of news in the *Defender*, the use of big headlines in red ink, and other attention-getting devices. He also kept close to the common people so that he might express in his pages their wants and desires. And, even after he became a wealthy man, he could be found mingling with stockyard workers and steel mill stokers on Chicago's South Side, listening to their problems concerning decent housing, prejudice in promotions, or segregation in unions. Because the *Defender* was for many years the leading newspaper of the Negro masses, it became known all over the country, and has had a very great influence on democratic thinking.

After Mr. Abbott's death *The Chicago Defender* continued under the editorship of his nephew, John H. Sengstacke. During World War II, while pressing for the complete abolition of segregation and discrimination in the armed forces and in industry, at the same time it carried many patriotic editorials in support of the War and conducted vigorous War Bond drives. One of its editorials in 1944 said:

> "Regardless of how deeply we may resent numerous injustices perpetrated against us and how hard we may fight against them, we must admit that this is our war too. Our boys are fighting overseas, facing a dangerous, murderous enemy who will destroy them and us as quickly as he will our white brothers. . . . Participation in this Fourth War Loan drive is not only a patriotic act, but is a matter of self interest."

Chicago's Negro community bought two million dollars worth of bonds. In honor of the newspaper that sponsored this campaign, the United States Maritime Commission named a newly built Liberty ship, launched at San Francisco, the U. S. S. *Robert S. Abbott*.

During his lifetime, Mr. Abbott became the National Executive President of the Hampton Alumni Association, a trustee of the Y.M.C.A., a member of the Board of Directors of the National Urban League, and a Life Member of the Field Museum. Now each year in Chicago a Memorial Award is given in his honor to someone who has made a distinguished contribution toward better race relations in America, and in 1945 *The Chicago Defender* established the Robert S. Abbott Memorial Scholarship at the Lincoln University School of Journalism. Meanwhile *The Chicago Defender* has extended its activities to include a chain of seven other newspapers from New York to Memphis.

PAUL LAURENCE DUNBAR

PAUL LAURENCE DUNBAR

The Robert Burns of Negro Poetry

Born 1872—Died 1906

Paul Laurence Dunbar's father was an escaped slave who took the Underground Railroad to Canada, but returned to fight as an enlisted soldier in the Civil War. He married a woman who had been a slave in Kentucky. Seven years after the War ended, a son was born to them at Dayton, Ohio. His father said, "We will name him Paul after the Apostle Paul in the Bible, because this boy is going to be a great man." His father did not live to see this happen. He died when Paul was only twelve years old. But his prophecy came true. Paul Laurence Dunbar did become a great man.

His mother could not read when Paul was born but, after her marriage, she had begun to learn, and she took pains to send her son to school as soon as he was old enough. As a widow she had to earn her own living, so she took in washing and ironing. Paul called for the soiled clothes and delivered the clean ones to her customers each week. At night together he and his mother studied spelling and young Paul was able to help her learn to write. But with all the work she had to do, she never did learn very well. And once, after her son was grown and away in another city, when a neighbor stopped by her house one morning, she said, "I must hurry up and get my washing done early because I have a hard day's work ahead of me."

The friend inquired, "What have you got to do?"

"I've got to write a letter to my son," said Mrs. Dunbar.

When Paul was graduated from high school, the only Negro in his class, as president of the literary society, he was chosen to write the Class Song to be sung at the graduation exercises. Since the age of seven he had been

85

writing little poems, and he had continued to write in high school where he became editor of the school paper. At thirteen he recited one of his own verses at an Easter Sunday school program. He was sixteen when his first printed poems appeared in *The Dayton Herald.* One of his high school English teachers was so impressed with Paul's talent for rhyming that, after his graduation, when the Western Association of Writers was meeting in Dayton, she arranged for him to compose a poem of welcome and recite it himself. Young Paul was then running an elevator in the Callahan Building on Main Street for a salary of $4.00 a week. He had to beg off from work for a few hours to attend the meeting. The assembled writers were astonished to see a young Negro lad walk to the platform at the opening of their session and greet them in poetry. But they were so impressed with his verses that when the meeting was over many sought to find him. No one in the hall could locate Paul, however, because he had gone back to work. But some of the writers finally found him running the elevator and congratulated him on his poem.

When Paul felt that he had enough poems for a book, he put them together and carried his manuscript to a small publishing house in Dayton where he was informed that poetry was a risky business and that only if he underwrote the cost of publication, could they bring out his poems. This would be $125.00. Young Paul did not have a dollar in the world, so he was about to turn away in disappointment when the business manager, who had heard about his talent, called him. Finally this man agreed personally to pay the costs if Paul would reimburse him from the first books sold. Paul gave his word and the little volume, *Oak and Ivy,* appeared in time for Christmas, 1893. Within two weeks, at a dollar each, Paul had sold enough copies to people who went up and down in his elevator to repay the publication costs. And the Reverend R. C. Ransom, who later became a bishop of the African Methodist Church, sold a hundred copies for Paul at his Sunday services.

That year the World's Columbian Exposition opened in Chicago, and Frederick Douglass was in charge of an exhibit from Haiti. Paul went to Chicago seeking better paying work. Douglass gave him a job at $5.00 a

Paul Laurence Dunbar

week as one of his assistants, and on Colored American Day both Dunbar and Douglass appeared on the same platform. When the Exposition was over Paul returned to Dayton and worked as a page boy at the Court House. The well-known James Whitcomb Riley had somehow heard of Paul's poems, and wrote him a letter of encouragement. As a reader of his own verses, Paul had begun to acquire some reputation in Dayton and surrounding towns, so the head of the State Hospital for the Insane, Dr. H. A. Tobey, arranged for the young man to have a program in Toledo. Its success brought Paul many new friends and through these his second volume, *Majors and Minors*, was privately printed in Toledo in 1895. On Paul's twenty-fourth birthday a famous American writer, William Dean Howells, reviewed this book enthusiastically in *Harper's Weekly*, a widely read national publication, devoting to it an entire page. It was this review that made Paul Laurence Dunbar nationally known almost over night. When the article appeared, Paul and his mother were away from home for a few days. On their return he found more than two hundred letters the mailman had stuck through the shutters of the front window. Many of the letters contained money orders for his new book.

Invitations to recite his poems soon came to Dunbar from a number of cities. Many of his verses were in the quaint and charming broken English of the newly freed slaves, such as his mother and father had spoken. Dunbar read these poems very well. And sometimes he even acted them out. When he recited *The Cornstalk Fiddle:*

> "Take your lady and balance down the middle,
> To the merry strains of the cornstalk fiddle. . . ."

he would himself dance the figures of an old-time country dance. Audiences loved him. Soon he had a manager to take charge of his engagements. In New York this manager arranged for him to see the big publishers, Dodd, Mead & Company, who in 1896 brought out the first of his books to be published by a real publishing house. For this volume, *Lyrics of Lowly Life*, William Dean Howells wrote the Introduction. The following year, that of Queen Victoria's Diamond Jubilee, young Dunbar went to London to read his poems. There he was well received, but his manager kept almost all the money so Paul had to cable friends in America for his return fare.

Always an industrious young man, while in London, instead of sightseeing much, he wrote his first novel, *The Uncalled*, which he sold to a magazine as a serial before it appeared in book form. John Hay, the American Ambassador to the Court of St. James, arranged a program for Paul in London and there he met many distinguished people. Just as the English, more than a hundred years before, had welcomed the Negro poet from Boston, Phillis Wheatley, so now they welcomed Paul Laurence Dunbar from Dayton. Luncheons, teas, and banquets were given in his honor, and he was a guest of the secretary of the Royal Geological Society. At that time many upper class Englishmen wore monocles, so Paul wrote home that in London, "the men, poor fellows, did not have enough eye-glasses to go around, so each had *one* stuck in the corner of his eye."

Before he went to London, Dunbar had fallen in love with a beautiful girl from New Orleans who had run away from home to see him off on the boat. So when he returned to America he wanted to get married. Therefore, he thought he should settle down and take a regular job. With the aid of Colonel Robert G. Ingersoll, he obtained a position as an assistant in the Reading Room of the Library of Congress in Washington at a salary of $750.00 a year. During his first months there he wrote a series of short stories for *Cosmopolitan*, later published in book form under the title, *Folks From Dixie*, dedicated to the Toledo doctor who had helped him get started. In Washington he got married, had a fine wedding, and Paul and his bride began to buy a cottage. Perhaps it was then that he wrote:

A little dreaming by the way,
A little toiling day by day;
A little pain, a little strife,
A little joy—and that is life.

A little short-lived summer's morn
When joy seems all so newly born,
When one day's sky is blue above,
And one bird sings—and that is love.

Paul Laurence Dunbar

For a few months they were very happy—but a few months only—then Paul began to feel badly and to cough a great deal. At first they thought the cough came from the dust on the books at the Library where he worked. But eventually Dunbar learned that he had tuberculosis.

Failing health forced him to resign from the Library of Congress, and for the next eight years he fought against his illness. There were periods when he could do nothing, followed by periods of intense activity. He wrote several more books of poetry and of prose. He read his poems in many cities. At the invitation of Booker T. Washington, he visited Tuskegee more than once and lectured to English classes there. Booker T. asked Paul to write a poem for an annual farmers' conference. He did, and read it to the assembled farmers. He also wrote the *Tuskegee Song* for the 25th Anniversary of that famous school:

> ".... The fields smile to greet us, the forests are glad,
> The ring of the anvil and hoe
> Have a music as thrilling and sweet as a harp
> Which thou taught us to hear and know...."

A student chorus of fifteen hundred voices sang it. The students at Negro schools and colleges all over the South had begun to read Dunbar's poems and to love them. While he was ill in New York in 1899, Atlanta University awarded him an honorary degree. But the poet could not go South for the ceremonies. He had instead to go West to the Rocky Mountains for his health. Ill though he was, he did not stop writing. In a cottage near Denver he finished another novel, *The Love of Landry*, laid in Colorado.

Although Paul Laurence Dunbar wrote a great deal of prose—four novels, four volumes of short stories, and many articles—and this work appeared in the best magazines and was widely read, it was his poetry that made him famous, that continued to be read after his death, and that is loved today. Many of his poems have been set to music. Especially for the delightful Negro composer, Will Marion Cook, in 1898 Dunbar wrote the lyrics for a musical sketch, *Clorindy—The Origin of the Cakewalk*, which was performed for an entire season at a popular New York music hall. Many of Dunbar's most beautiful poems were written in straight English. But his most popular and charming ones are in the old-time Negro dialect of a sort no longer spoken and rather hard for people to read today. Yet the charm and the humor are still there behind the broken English of that difficult period following the Civil War when a whole race of people was still trying to learn to read and write:

> "Little brown baby wif spa'klin' eyes,
> Come to yo' pappy an' set on his knee.
> What you been doin', suh,—makin' san' pies?
> Look at dat bib—you's ez du'ty ez me.
> Look at dat mouf—dat's merlasses, I bet;
> Come hyeah, Maria, an' wipe off his han's.
> Bees gwine to ketch you an' eat you up yit,
> Bein' so sticky an' sweet—goodness lan's!'"

When Paul Laurence Dunbar died in Dayton in 1906 his friend, the Mayor of Toledo, Brand Whitlock, wrote:

> "Nature, who knows so much better than man about everything invariably seizes the opportunity to show her contempt of rank and title and race and land and creed. She took Burns from a plow and Paul from an elevator, and Paul has done for his own people what Burns did for the peasants of Scotland—he has expressed them in their own way and in their own words. . . . There was nothing foreign in Paul's poetry, nothing imported, nothing imitated: it was all original, native, and indigenous. Thus he becomes the poet not of his own race alone—I wish I could make people see this—but the poet of you and of me and of all men everywhere."

Paul Laurence Dunbar was buried on Lincoln's Birthday, and hundreds of people attended his funeral. Beside his grave his mother planted a willow tree, for the site had been selected to correspond to the setting Paul had described in his poem, *A Death Song*, when he wrote:

Paul Laurence Dunbar

"Lay me down beneaf de willers in de grass,
  Whah de branch'll go a-singin' as it pass.
      An' w'en I's a-layin' low,
      I kin hyeah it as it go
Singin', 'Sleep, my honey, tek yo' res' at las'.'"

W. C. HANDY

W. C. HANDY

Father of the Blues

Born 1873—

HOTEL ORCHESTRAS in Europe frequently strike up *The St. Louis Blues* when they learn that there are American guests in the dining room. Around the world this blues has long been the best known American popular song and the one most often played. Some foreigners are even under the mistaken impression that it is the American National Anthem. During World War II when Hitler's armies invaded France and American jazz music was forbidden on the government radio in Paris, the French continued to play *The St. Louis Blues*, anyway, calling it *La Tristesse de Saint Louis*. When the German censors asked if it was not an American Negro song, the French said, "Oh, my no! Don't you know this song really goes much farther back than that? The man in the song is King Louis the Fourteenth, and the woman with the diamond rings is in truth Marie Antoinette. What a sad ending she had! *Quelle tristesse!*"

The man who wrote *The St. Louis Blues* was born in Florence, Alabama, near the Muscle Shoals Canal, eight years after the Civil War. He was christened William Christopher Handy, in the church which his grandfather had built on a hill called, because his folks had lived there so long, Handy's Hill. All around the house were orchards of peaches, pears, cherries and plums where birds and butterflies fluttered, lightening bugs glowed in the evenings, and hoot owls sometimes roosted. Not far off were meadows where cattle grazed. And in the bogs and along the canal banks bullfrogs croaked and snakes coiled and hissed. One morning when little William's mother came to wake him up, she found a snake sleeping in the bed with her child.

Certainly his early life was spent close to nature. And he was particularly fascinated by the music in the bird calls, the cricket chirps, and lowing of the cattle, and the night cries of owls and frogs.

When William started to school, his favorite class was music. It was his good fortune to have a young man teacher just out of Fisk University who every morning devoted the first half hour of school to singing, without the aid of piano for they had none. This teacher was a lover of great music. He taught the children not only all the gospel hymns, but excerpts from the operas of Wagner, Verdi, and Bizet. He drilled them thoroughly in their scales and in sight reading. Young Handy began to fit what he learned in school to what he heard in the woodlands, searching around in his mind for notes to correspond to those the birds sang or the katydids chirped. Even the mooing of a cow seemed to him to have melody in it, and years later he wrote a piece called the *Honking Cow Blues*.

But music to his father, a Methodist minister, was something only for church and school. And musical instruments to him were taboo—"instruments of Satan." He did not even permit a piano or an organ in his church. But, nevertheless, little Handy was playing tunes on a fine-tooth comb, or beating out rhythms on his mother's tin pans, or trying to reproduce on a mouth organ the cotton field melodies that he heard rising in the sun-light. And once he tried to make a trumpet from a cow's horn, but it would blow only one note. When he was twelve years old, he got a job as a water boy in a rock quarry near Muscle Shoals at fifty cents a day. There he heard the wonderfully rhythmical songs of the steel-drivers at work:

"There ain't no hammer. . . . Huh!
That-a rings like mine, boys. . . . Huh!"

grunting in unison as the hammers fell. It was then that he began to save his money to buy a guitar that he had seen in a window downtown. Finally he had enough cash. But when he came home with the instrument, his father and mother were so shocked they could hardly speak. They called the guitar "one of the devil's playthings," and ordered him to take it out of their house at once. In fact, they made him return it to the department store where he

W. C. Handy

had purchased it and exchange the guitar for something he could use in school—a *Webster's Dictionary.*

In those days in the South actors and musicians as a class were considered trifling people. But it seemed very difficult to teach little Handy that this might be so. One day in school the teacher was asking each member of William's class what careers they intended to follow. Some said lawyers, some said doctors, some nurses, some teachers. When it came his turn he said, "A musician." His teacher was so horrified that he not only scolded him roundly in front of the whole class, but wrote his father a note. That night William's father said that he had rather follow his coffin to the grave than to see him turn out a worthless musician. This had no effect upon the son, especially after a wonderful fiddle player named Jim Turner came to town. Turner was from Memphis where his sweetheart had quit him, leaving him so brokenhearted that he simply went down to the station, pulled out his money, and asked the agent for a ticket to anywhere—just *anywhere* away from there. The agent sold him a ticket to Florence. On his violin Turner could play wonderful waltzes, minuets, mazurkas, and schottishes that fascinated young Handy and made him more determined than ever to be a musician.

A while later a circus was stranded in Florence and its bandmaster, in order to make some quick money, began to give band instructions at night in a colored barber shop. William stood outside the window looking and listening and learning, although he had no instrument on which to play and no money to pay for lessons. One of the members of the band sold him an old cornet for a dollar and seventy-five cents and showed him how to finger the valves. Then William would stand outside the barber shop blowing on this while the men inside practiced with their teacher. Finally they let him come inside and rehearse with the band. Once they needed a player for an out-of-town engagement, so he played hookey from school and went along. He earned eight dollars of which he thought his father would be proud. But no, he was not! And he got a whipping besides from his teacher for missing classes.

When the famous Georgia Minstrels came to town Handy was so impressed by the band, the singers, and comedians like Billy Kersands (who could put a whole cup and saucer in his mouth) that he joined a home-town minstrel show himself and sang tenor in the quartet. When he was in his teens this group went on a tour and got stranded in Jasper, Alabama, where the boys had to sing for their suppers and walk part of the way back home to Florence. His father, frowning on these activities, wanted him to be a minister. Instead young Handy decided to be a teacher. So when he came out of school he took the County Teacher's Examination in Birmingham and got the second highest mark. But when he found out that teachers' salaries were even less than a dollar a day, he decided instead to go to work at a foundry in Bessemer. While there he organized a brass band, a string orchestra, and, on Sundays, played a trumpet in the church choir. But a depression came and he lost his job, the main source of income. Meanwhile, he had organized a quartet and, hearing that there was to be a World's Fair in Chicago that year, the four young men decided to hobo there on a freight train. The brakeman soon put the boys off on a lonely stretch of railroad track in the dark of night. The poor fellows started singing there beside the track. They sang so mournfully that the brakeman took pity on them and let them get back in a box car and ride into Decatur. Handy had twenty cents, so the next morning he bought a loaf of bread and some molasses and sat down beside a spring for breakfast. While they were eating they saw an excursion boat docking and a group of ladies going on board for a picnic outing. Handy ran up and presented them with one of his handwritten cards, *The Lauzetta Quartet,* and the ladies hired them on the spot to sing as they sailed down the Tennessee River. For this the boys got ten dollars and all they could eat from the picnic baskets. Finally, they reached Chicago—only to find that the World's Fair had been postponed for a year.

St. Louis at that time was said to be a very lively town, so they headed there. But it was then in the throes of the depression, too, and nobody had any extra money for music, so the quartet broke up. Jobs were hard to find. Handy slept in the hay of the horses' stalls at the race track and sometimes on the levee of the Mississippi River with thousands of other penniless men.

W. C. Handy

Then he discovered a big pool hall on Targee Street where you could sit and sleep so long as the police did not bother you. He was told that the way the police judged if a man was asleep or not was by whether his feet were moving. Handy learned to sleep with one foot swinging all the time. Sometimes a one-eyed man slept with his hat over his sleeping eye while his glass eye, wide open, was exposed—to fool the cops. The police carried long night-sticks that they loved to use, so nobody wanted to be taken as a vagrant. But neither do homeless men like to be outdoors in the damp of evening. And when it is cold, they dread the coming of nightfall. From his experiences in St. Louis years later Handy derived the opening line of his famous blues:

"I hate to see the evenin' sun go down...."

But he was too proud to go back home to hear his father say, "I told you so! Ruination! Musicians, nothing but bums!"

So Handy did not go home. He hit the road as a freight-train rider again, and found himself one day in Evansville, Indiana, where he got work with a street paving gang. In a little while he was playing with a local band there. One day he went to Henderson, Kentucky, to play for a barbecue. He liked beautiful green Kentucky so well that he stayed, met his wife there, and got a job as a janitor at Liederkranz Hall where a wonderful German singing society rehearsed—just so he could learn from its rehearsals. Meanwhile, he continued to play nights in a little band. One of the musicians from this band had joined Mahara's Colored Minstrels and, when he learned that they needed a new cornet player, he wrote Handy to join the troup. He did in 1896, and from that time on he was a professional musician.

As a child, his grandmother had always told him that since he had big ears, he must have a talent for music. She was right, for, as a part of a touring minstrel show, his musical abilities developed in many ways, and he became of great value to the troup, playing solo leads, making arrangements of new tunes, and training quartets. Within a year this talented young man had been made the leader of a thirty-piece parade band, and conducted the forty-two-piece ensemble for the pre-curtain concerts in the evening.

For the next four years Handy traveled all over the United States and Canada and into Mexico and Cuba with the minstrels. But, having a little daughter by now, he thought he should settle down, so he took a job as a teacher of music and English at Alabama Agricultural and Mechanical College near Huntsville, Alabama. But the pay was only $40.00 a month, the duties were heavy and worst of all, the president liked only hymns and "classics"—"classics" meaning European compositions. By this time Handy had learned how much audiences all over the land enjoyed American popular music and ragtime. But he was not permitted to teach or play such music at the college. So one day he decided to fool them with his student band. He took a piece called *My Ragtime Baby* and changed the title to *Greetings to Toussaint L'Ouverture, the Liberator of Haiti,* and so it was announced on the printed programs of a college celebration. Not only the students, but the faculty, applauded loudly when the piece was over. They enjoyed it immensely. But, when he told the faculty of the joke he had played on them, it was not appreciated at all. Handy did not remain long at Alabama A. & M. He rejoined the Mahara's Minstrels, and became their star cornet soloist and conductor.

When motion picture theaters began to open up all over the country the minstrels, a form of American entertainment popular for over fifty years, began to decline. The thirty-year-old Handy, with a second child by now, decided to accept the post of bandmaster with the Knights of Pythias Band in Clarksdale, Mississippi. In this city deep in the cotton lands of the Delta, not far from the river, on Saturday nights cotton pickers, roustabouts, and levee camp workers came to town. Handy's band, or the orchestra that he organized from it, made frequent trips into the country to play for picnics or dances. In a region rich with song, he heard the minor melodies of the fields and the river, the Negro work-songs, jail-house songs, and unwritten blues that were shortly to form the basis for his own compositions. The members of his band and orchestra were all trained musicians, playing by note, and inclined to conventional music. They came mostly from religious homes where playing music was not too highly thought of, anyway, and ragtime and minstrel songs were considered sinful. So by preference they

100

W. C. Handy

played mostly the standard marches and the more sedate waltzes and two-steps.

But one night, playing for a dance in Cleveland, Mississippi, Handy was asked if he would mind if a trio of local roustabouts contributed a few numbers. Happy to have a rest for his men, he gave the platform up to a group of ragged youngsters who began an endless but very rhythmical tune on their battered string instruments that soon had the whole crowd dancing, swaying, and clapping hands as Handy's own band had not been able to make them do all evening. When the piece was over, the crowd cried for more, and showered the untrained musicians with silver dollars and smaller coins. In the end these boys picked up more money than the Handy band was paid for the whole evening. And the tunes they played were nothing more than those heard every day in the cotton fields and on the levee. That night Handy was more than ever convinced of the pleasure people might find in our own American Negro music, and in the syncopated way in which untrained musicians sang and played.

It was in Memphis where he had moved to take charge of a band, that Handy had a chance to try out this conviction during a political campaign. There were three candidates for mayor, and each faction hired a band to play at political rallies. Handy's band was employed to back Edward H. Crump who later became a great power in Memphis politics. Handy wrote a campaign tune for Mr. Crump, based on his memories of the rhythms of the uneducated Negroes. Immediately this composition swept Memphis. White and colored people danced in the streets when it was played. Handy received so many requests for his band to perform in so many places at the same time, that he had to break the band up into several small units. His tune, *Mr. Crump*, with its levee swing and cotton field slurs, was a hit. Mr. Crump himself was elected Mayor of Memphis. And W. C. Handy, as he was known, became famous throughout the Delta. Soon he organized more bands, and all of them were kept busy playing in Memphis or nearby towns. After the campaign was over, the title, *Mr. Crump*, he changed to *The Memphis Blues*. Thus the first famous American blues came into being.

The Memphis Blues was published in 1912. But Handy, not realizing its value, had sold his rights to it for $50.00. So, as its popularity spread across the country, others made thousands of dollars from it while he got nothing. But the tune made him very well known as a song writer, so he determined to follow it up with more compositions. Having by now four children, Handy found it very difficult to compose at home. One night he rented a room over a saloon on Beale Street and stayed up all night writing a new song. The song came out of his deepest memories; the rock quarry melodies of his youth, hoboing on the railroad, tramping from place to place, town to town; the homeless nights in St. Louis when he hated to see the sun go down; a woman he heard once complaining that her lover had a heart as hard as a rock cast in the sea; the women in St. Louis with their diamond rings; the river songs he had heard on the levee. Out of those memories *The St. Louis Blues* was born. The next day he orchestrated it. That night he played it at a dance. The dancers loved it, applauded and applauded, whistled, stamped their feet, and demanded that it be played again and again.

For two days Handy had not been home. When, after the dance, he rushed to the house to tell his wife about his new hit, she met him with a rolling pin! He sang:

> "Saint Louis Blues,
> Just as blue as I can be...."

"Blue, nothing!" his wife said. "I'm the one who ought to be blue. Why didn't you tell me you intended to stay away from home like this? Where have you been?"

Mrs. Handy was not excited about the new song at all, not that night. She was angry. Of course, she and W. C. Handy were both very happy later when thousands of dollars in royalties from sheet music and record sales of *The St. Louis Blues* started to come in. Almost all the leading popular singers and big bands began to record the song. One day the mailman dropped at Handy's house in Memphis a copy of the latest Victor Records catalogue. In running his eye down the list of composers under the letter *H* he saw:

W. C. Handy

Handel
Handy
Hayden

His name between the names of two of the great masters! When he showed it to his children they said, "Papa, who's them other two men?"

The St. Louis Blues has had over four hundred different recordings. New ones are continually being made not only in English, but in other languages all over the world. From Okinawa during World War II some soldiers sent W. C. Handy a Japanese record they had found in a dugout there of *The St. Louis Blues*, sung in Japanese. Ordinary people and royalty alike have loved the song. King Edward VIII had his Scottish bagpipers play this blues at Balmoral Castle. *Life* magazine reported it as Queen Elizabeth's favorite piece of dance music. Since the 369th Infantry Band introduced it to Europe during the First World War, this blues is said to have influenced the work of such modern composers as Stravinsky, Honnegger, and Milhaud. And certainly it influenced George Gershwin, as he himself acknowledged, in his writing of such famous American works as the *Rhapsody in Blue* and *Porgy and Bess*. John Alden Carpenter wrote a symphonic blues, *Katnip Blues*. There have been hundreds of composers who have tried their hand at straight blues or popular songs in the blues style: Hoagy Carmichael's *Washboard Blues*, Clarence Williams' *Basin Street Blues*, Johnny Mercer's *Blues in the Night*, Harold Arlen's *Stormy Weather*. Dorothy Lamour appeared in a motion picture called *The St. Louis Blues*, as did Bessie Smith in an earlier short film of the same title. From tiny night clubs to Madison Square Garden, from river boats to Broadway theaters, juke boxes to films, radio to TV, *The St. Louis Blues* has been sung. Perhaps one of the largest audiences to hear it at one time was at a *Chicago Tribune* Music Festival in Soldiers Field when a massed chorus of three thousand voices sang it to an audience of 125,000 people.

W. C. Handy was forty years old when he wrote this song that started him on the road to fame and fortune. Since that time he has become an established music publisher on Broadway, heading the largest Negro publishing firm in the country. He has played his golden horn in all the leading theaters of America, at the International Exposition on Treasure Island in San Francisco, and at the New York World's Fair. He has appeared on every major radio and television network many times. At the age of sixty he toured America with Joe Laurie, Jr.'s *Memory Lane* Company, playing his own blues. Even after he lost his eyesight, Mr. Handy was appearing nightly at Billy Rose's Diamond Horseshoe in New York playing *The St. Louis Blues* as a solo on the cornet. He has composed a great many songs and instrumental compositions, arranged hundreds of others, edited musical anthologies, and compiled a fascinating autobiography, *Father of the Blues*. He was over seventy and entirely blind when he accidentally fell on his head from the platform onto the subway tracks in New York City. For a few days everybody thought he was going to die. But he recovered and returned to his Broadway office and his theater, radio, and TV work.

He was one of the organizers of the Negro Actors Guild. He is also a founder of the W. C. Handy Foundation for the Blind. For a number of years his annual birthday dinners at some large New York hotel have brought in sizable sums for this worthy charity. Now there is a park in Memphis named after him. On the very spot where he slept hungry and penniless as a young man the city of St. Louis is planning a memorial tower with a clock which will chime *The St. Louis Blues*. And in Florence, Alabama, where he was born, there is a beautiful new W. C. Handy School, in honor of the man who has been such a great influence on modern American music—and who first, as a child, began to learn the beauties of our music from the rock quarry and cotton field melodies of his native Alabama.

CHARLES C. SPAULDING

CHARLES C. SPAULDING

Executive of World's Largest Negro Business

Born 1874—Died 1952

THE YEARS IMMEDIATELY following Emancipation were very difficult ones for the newly freed but destitute Negroes. Often they could not afford medical care for the sick, or even to bury the dead. So, to do these things, they had to band together. Therefore, many fraternal groups, mutual benefit organizations, and burial societies came into being, a number of them connected with or growing out of the churches. Even before the War between the States some such groups had been formed among the Negroes of the North. The Free African Society founded in 1787 in Philadelphia was organized "to support one another in sickness, and for the benefit of their widows and fatherless children." Such fraternal lodges as the Masons, the Elks, the Odd Fellows, and the Independent Order of St. Luke founded by a newly freed woman in 1867 and still in successful operation, had the same objectives. The first Negro-owned insurance, the African Insurance Company, started in 1810 with a capital of $5,000. Today insurance is the largest American Negro business with more than two hundred companies owned and operated entirely by colored people. Their combined insurance in force amounts to more than a billion dollars.

The largest Negro insurance firm in the world is the North Carolina Mutual Life Insurance Company of Durham, North Carolina. Charles Clinton Spaulding was, until his death in 1952, its president. His connection with the company began as its first manager in 1898, and he saw it grow from the ground up. Spaulding had no experience in insurance when he went into the formation of the concern, so he had to learn from scratch. And he had only an eighth grade education as a background. After he became wealthy and famous in the business world, he often said, "The only time I have ever been to college was to deliver a Commencement address."

Spaulding was born on a farm in Columbus County, North Carolina, nine years after Abraham Lincoln was assassinated. He was the third in a family of fourteen children, and being one of the oldest, much of the farm work fell to him. His attendance at school was irregular so, when he became a man, he decided to leave the plow and go to Durham and make a determined effort to at least get through grammar school. In the city Charles got a job at $10.00 a month as a dishwasher in a hotel, and later he became a bellboy in the evenings so he could attend classes by day. He was then twenty-one years old and much too big to be in grammar school with younger boys. But he swallowed his pride and went anyway, finishing the eighth grade—which was as far as Negro boys could go in Durham—at the age of twenty-three. About that time a group of colored men started a grocery store by putting in $25.00 each. They asked Charles Spaulding to be its clerk and manager. None of them had any experience in business, the store soon went broke, and everyone pulled out leaving Spaulding with debts of over $300.00. It took him five years to pay off these debts, but he paid every cent.

Spaulding's integrity and industry attracted the attention of a successful Negro barber, John Merrick, who owned five barber shops in Durham, three for white patrons and two for Negroes, and who was the personal barber to Washington Duke, founder of the American Tobacco Company. Mr. Merrick was interested in starting an insurance company. Dr. A. M. Moore, an uncle of Spaulding's, was interested, too. They both were very busy men so they asked young Spaulding to be the manager. Since he became the only member of the actual working staff, this meant that he also had to be the bookkeeper, typist, field agent, office boy and janitor. His headquarters were a back room in Dr. Moore's office. He once said, "When I came into the office in the morning, I rolled up my sleeves and swept the place as janitor. Then I rolled down my sleeves and was an agent. And later I put on my coat and became the general manager." He was indeed the man of all work.

The first client of the new insurance company was a man who paid 65¢ as

108

Charles C. Spaulding

the initial premium on a $40.00 policy. Then he promptly died a few days later—before the new company had had a chance to build up any additional funds. When his widow came to claim the insurance, the backers had to dig down into their own pockets to pay the $40.00. But they paid it. Word spread of the promptness and the solvency of the new firm. So young Spaulding did not find it too difficult to sign other policy holders. The first week's income was $29.40. By the end of the year he had taken in $840.00. Not even a thousand, but he was not discouraged because every week, though slowly, the number of policy holders grew. Into the small towns nearby and onto the farms he went, explaining to people the benefits of insurance—who had never heard of insurance before. Twenty years later, when he became secretary-treasurer of the company, his field agents were turning in annually more than a million dollars.

John Merrick, the barber, was the president of the company for twenty-one years. When he died, Dr. Moore succeeded him. Between them they did many good things for the Negro citizens of Durham. Colored people could not get books from the public library, so the two contributed substantially to the creation of a Colored Public Library and Dr. Moore himself gave many of the first books. Since Negro doctors and nurses could not serve on the staff of the City Hospital, they persuaded the wealthy Duke family to aid in the building of Lincoln Hospital for colored patients, where young colored doctors might interne, and nurses be trained. Remembering the bad conditions he had encountered in the rural schools, Dr. Moore personally paid for a year the salary of an inspector of Negro schools so that he might make recommendations to the Legislature for improvements. So successful was the inspector's work that the next year the State made the inspector's position permanent.

When these two good men who founded the North Carolina Mutual Insurance Company died, Charles C. Spaulding carried on their community work in the same spirit of civic responsibility. He not only built the insurance company into one of the most important in America, but he kept up many varied outside interests as well. In 1921 he helped to organize the National Negro Insurance Association and was its first president. In 1926 he became the president of the National Negro Business League. He served as a trustee of the universities of Howard, Shaw, and of the North Carolina State College. He was a member of the National Council of the Young Men's Christian Association, and of the Durham Chamber of Commerce. He was awarded a number of honorary degrees. And in 1926 he received the Harmon Gold Award for Distinguished Achievement.

Out of the North Carolina Mutual Company grew two other major businesses in Durham, the Mechanics and Farmers Bank, and the Mutual Building and Loan Association. In the 1920's Charles C. Spaulding became president of both. One of the purposes Merrick and Moore had in mind when they started their insurance was to provide young Negroes with opportunities to get business training. They wanted also to set up various enterprises where young men and women might get white collar jobs of a sort not generally open to Negroes in the South. They knew, too, that it was very difficult for colored people to get loans on property or secure help in financing the building of homes. To that end they opened their bank, as well as a finance association.

When Charles C. Spaulding died in 1952 *The New York Herald Tribune* reported that the North Carolina Mutual Life Insurance Company with its affiliates was the largest all-Negro business enterprise in the world, having assets of more than thirty-three million dollars, and over 165 million dollars worth of insurance policies in force in eight states. A very modest man, and a firm believer in Booker T. Washington's advice to let down your bucket where you are, Spaulding laid his success entirely to hard work. He had great faith in personal initiative. In giving advice to young people, he often said, "You can't drink from the spring high up on the mountain unless you climb for the water."

A. PHILIP RANDOLPH

A. PHILIP RANDOLPH

Distinguished Labor Leader

Born 1889—

THE FIRST Pullman car in America was named the "Pioneer." And its first porter was a Negro. Since 1867 colored sleeping car porters have been working on all the railroads in the United States. Today they number about 18,000. Most of them belong to the Brotherhood of Sleeping Car Porters, the largest Negro labor union in the world. This union was organized by Asa Philip Randolph.

Randolph was born in Crescent City, Florida, April 15, 1889, the son of a traveling Methodist preacher with several rural churches to pastor. There was a good library of religious literature in the home and, as he grew up, young Randolph used to practice reading aloud from his father's volumes of famous sermons and from Shakespeare's plays. In school he was a good student, but not a brilliant one, and his regular schooling ended with a high school diploma from Cookman Institute in Jacksonville. After he was graduated he decided to seek his fortune in the North, so Philip came to New York where he worked as a bus boy, then an elevator man, meanwhile taking a few night courses at City College. One summer he got a job as a waiter on the Hudson River boats, but was fired for attempting to organize a protest against the hot, crowded quarters allotted to the crew. From his early manhood he was interested in improving conditions for Negroes, especially working conditions, so he soon began to speak from soap boxes on the streets of Harlem. And sometimes he recited bits of Shakespeare to the passing crowds.

In Florida as a child his mother had always forbade her son to ride in the segregated street cars. She said it was better to walk than to be Jim

113

Crowed. So young Randolph was early imbued with an intense dislike of racial discrimination. In 1917 he helped to launch a magazine in New York called *The Messenger* to crusade for the full democratic rights of Negro citizens. Beneath its title was printed, "The Only Radical Negro Magazine in America," and its editorials were bitterly critical of the *status quo*. During World War I it criticized as hypocritical the official slogan, "Making the World Safe for Democracy," while, so *The Messenger* contended, Negro citizens were disfranchised, segregated, and lynched throughout the South. Randolph made very fiery speeches in a number of cities. In 1918 some newspapers termed him "the most dangerous Negro in America," and he was arrested for a talk which he made in Cleveland. But a few days later he was released without being brought to trial. In his talks and editorials Randolph contended he was simply agitating for the fulfillment of our Constitutional guarantees for *all* citizens and the protection of the law for everybody. One of the things he said in his speeches was, "Rights do not mean anything if you cannot exercise them."

After the war Randolph entered politics on the Socialist ticket and ran for a number of public offices without success. Meanwhile, he was in great demand as a speaker before Negro groups and, as such, one night he was invited to the Pullman Porters Athletic Association where he discussed the growing importance in American life of trade unionism. As a result of his address, a group of porters and maids on the trains asked his help in organizing a union. Four times before in various parts of the country the porters had attempted to organize unions but had failed. The best they had achieved was a kind of low-benefit insurance association controlled by the company. But this had not shortened their long hours of work, nor given them sleeping quarters on the trains, nor raised their very low wages. Sleeping car porters were almost entirely dependent on tips for a living, had to pay for meals and lodging away from home, and even had to buy their own polish for shining passengers' shoes.

Randolph himself had never been a Pullman porter, but he had long been interested in labor organizations and in the theories and practices of unionism. He felt that it was high time one of the largest groups of Negro workers in

A. Philip Randolph

the country be unionized so, when the porters in the New York area invited him to become their general organizer, he went to work at first without a salary. In 1925 at a meeting in the Elks Hall in Harlem, the Brotherhood of Sleeping Car Porters was organized. At first the going was difficult. A number of porters lost their jobs for belonging to the union. A great many others were afraid to join. Some felt that, because many unions would not admit Negroes, no unions were any good. To spread the concepts and values of unionism, labor institutes were organized in the leading cities from Coast to Coast. Randolph traveled a great deal seeking to enlist members, create good will for the new Brotherhood, and explain to colored people the growing importance of labor organizations. He made many talks to religious groups, contending that the church could serve "nobly in championing the cause of labor and yet remain true to its traditions, since Jesus Christ was a carpenter and all his disciples workmen." His magazine, *The Messenger*, became "The Official Organ of the Brotherhood of Sleeping Car Porters." Within two years the new union grew to over two thousand members. But several thousand porters still remained to be organized. With a depression on its way and many people out of work, the fear of being discharged for union activities made many sleeping car workers reluctant to join the Brotherhood. Nevertheless, its membership continued to grow until by 1929 more than half of the porters and maids on the railroads were organized. Then the American Federation of Labor granted the Brotherhood of Sleeping Car Porters a charter—the first such charter to be given to an all-Negro union in America. A. Philip Randolph was its president.

During the depression the young union had such a hard time, with train crews being laid off and many of its members unable to pay dues, that it was not even able to meet its electric light bills. At its New York headquarters, officials had to work in the dark. But they continued to negotiate for better working conditions, and finally, in 1937, the Pullman Company signed an agreement with the Brotherhood which granted porters and maids an annual salary increase of over a million dollars, shorter working hours, less working mileage, and better overtime pay. This, remarkably enough, was achieved *without striking*. Today the Brotherhood of Sleeping Car Porters is considered one of the soundest labor organizations in the country. Of it Leo Wolman, Professor of Economics in Columbia University, has written, "The record of this union affords evidence, if any were needed, of the capacity of Negroes to run a large union democratically and to handle their relations with employers with common sense."

As a labor leader, A. Philip Randolph continued to increase in importance by his enlarged activities within the American Federation of Labor. At its annual conventions he sought to have those member unions that still barred Negro workers drop their color bars. He declared, "Labor can never win fully until its opens its doors freely and equally to all workers." But it was not until World War II when the federal government took a hand in this, that much headway was made. Because a large number of important defense industries would not employ colored men and women, and because many unions kept Negroes from working in the shops and plants, even before the War Randolph felt that forceful steps needed to be taken. To that end he decided to exercise the old American right of petition for "redress of grievances." He began to organize a protest demonstration of Negro citizens to go to Washington to appeal to the President and Congress to see that Negro workers be employed in defense plants on the same basis as others.

Many organizations, churches, lodges, and newspapers approved of his idea, and large mass meetings were held all across the country in support of what came to be called The March-on-Washington Movement. Hundreds of groups offered to send delegates to Washington, and by June, 1941, some fifty thousand colored citizens were expected to march to the White House with their petitions for "jobs and equal participation in national defense." Government officials began to understand that Negro citizens were very much in earnest and greatly concerned because many airplane factories and munitions plants preparing for the defense of democracy still would not employ them. Just a few days before the March-on-Washington was to have been held, President Roosevelt issued his Executive Order 8802 against discrimination in employment by firms holding defense contracts. This historic order stated in clear language that "it is the duty of employers and labor organizations . . . to provide for the full and equitable participation of all workers

A. Philip Randolph

in defense industries, without discrimination because of race, creed, color, or national origin." A Committee of Fair Employment Practices was formed in Washington to insure the rights of all citizens to take part in our national defense program. And a clause was written into government defense contracts prohibiting racial bias in employment.

The historian, John Hope Franklin, states in his book, *From Slavery to Freedom*, "Negroes hailed the Order as the most significant document affecting them since the issuance of the Emancipation Proclamation." But he further records that some firms defied the Order. Nevertheless, with governmental recognition and official condemnation of a difficulty that had long plagued Negro workers, the march on Washington was not held. Instead, 20,000 people met in New York's Madison Square Garden to hail Randolph's leadership and to pledge continued support to his efforts for full employment without discrimination. Certainly the doors of industry had been opened to colored workers in greater numbers than ever before. And A. Philip Randolph had moved on from a labor leader to a national leader in the eyes of the Negro people.

RALPH BUNCHE

RALPH BUNCHE

Statesman and Political Scientist

Born 1904—

IN ANCIENT TIMES Israel, before it was conquered by David, was called the Land of Canaan. Then, according to the Bible, "when David was old and full of days, he made Solomon, his son, king over Israel." Later the country was conquered by Babylon. Still later the Persians and the Macedonians overran it. Then when Jesus was born, Palestine was in the hands of the Romans. In time it came to be called the Holy Land, the name remaining even after the Roman Empire fell and it was taken over by the Mohammedans. During the Crusades the Islamic rulers were driven out, only to come back later to remain until the British took the Holy Land from the Turks during the First World War. The Jewish people in the twentieth century, fleeing from the pogroms and gas ovens of Nazi Europe, wanted to make Palestine their home. The Moslems resented this. So in 1936 serious conflicts began to develop between its mixed population of Jews and Arabs. When the Second World War was over, Great Britain dumped the whole problem of Palestine into the domain of the fledgling United Nations. And eventually it fell into the lap of a young American Negro diplomat at the U. N., Dr. Ralph Bunche. It was Dr. Bunche who brought about first a truce, then an armistice, and in 1949 the end of the Arab-Israeli conflict.

On August 7, 1904, Ralph Johnson Bunche was born in Detroit, Michigan, the son of a barber. He was born in an apartment over the barber shop where his parents, two aunts, and a grandmother lived. All the grown-ups worked, and, at an early age, Ralph began to sell papers to help along the family income. Grandma Johnson not only worked outside the home, but

121

seemed to be the mainstay in keeping everybody—her three daughters, two grandchildren, her son-in-law—and the house neat, clean, and straight. Grandma was the one who always had an extra dollar in her stocking when times got hard. And it was Grandma who took over when both of Ralph's parents became ill and the doctors thought they might get better if they went to the dry climate of the West.

The whole family—father, mother, Ralph and baby sister, two aunts, and Grandma—moved almost all the way across the country to the desert town of Albuquerque, New Mexico, in search of sunshine and dry air. At St. Louis, where the train headed into the South, for the first time little Ralph rode in a Jim Crow car set apart near the engine for Negro passengers. Half the coach was for baggage and the other half for Negroes. It was the first time Ralph had encountered legal segregation, so the boy was glad when the train got out of Texas and into New Mexico where there are no racial segregation laws. The mountains, the deserts, and the Indians of the Southwest thrilled eleven-year-old Ralph. He liked the sunny city and the new school he attended. But it was not long before his mother died of the rheumatic fever they had hoped the sunshine would cure. And only a few months later his father became weaker and weaker from tuberculosis. He died, too. Grandma accepted the job of rearing her two grandchildren. And the first thing she determined was that, no matter what happened, Ralph was to stay in school and get his education. In 1916 Grandma Johnson moved on to the West Coast. And two years later, Ralph was graduated from the elementary school in Los Angeles. Grandma came to the exercises to see him receive two prizes, one in History and one in English.

At Jefferson High School young Ralph went out for the debating team, and for football, basketball, baseball, and track. He was an all-around good athlete and a good student. By her earnings as a seamstress and a house-worker, his grandmother saw to it that Ralph had time for both sports and studies, and she was very proud of his achievements in high school. During the summers, Ralph worked hard and saved for school. One summer he worked in a carpet-dying plant; another he was houseboy for a Hollywood star; again he was a messenger in a newspaper office. Once, when the paper

Ralph Bunche

gave an outing for its employees, Ralph, of course, attended. But he was not allowed to go into the swimming pool because he was colored. These kinds of discriminations always perturbed him a great deal, and led directly to his early interest in sociology, civics, history, and other studies that might help to explain why democracy put so many stumbling blocks before its Negro citizens. When Ralph came out of high school, he received at graduation a medal for civics and one for debating.

Ralph began to think that perhaps he should now find a full-time job and go to work. But his grandmother said, "Young man, you are going to college." Her tone of voice meant just what she said. So he enrolled at the University of California at Los Angeles, where his athletic abilities in high school had earned him a four-year scholarship. But to make textbook money and spending change, he got a campus job as a gymnasium janitor, getting up at five to wax the floors and keep the mats, bars, rings, and track clean. All went well for a few months, then Ralph developed a mastoid condition from a tiny piece of straw that had worked its way into his ear on a picnic. Two operations, eventual deafness in one ear, and the loss of a whole year in college were the result. Nevertheless, in 1927, he was graduated *summa cum laude*, class valedictorian, and a member of Phi Beta Kappa. This graduation brought five medals for excellence in various studies, plus a scholarship for further work at Harvard University. The Negro community in Los Angeles had grown very proud of this brilliant young student and, before he started off to Harvard, they presented him with a fund of a thousand dollars to help defray his expenses. His grandmother, whose love and faith and toil had meant so much in getting him through school, died just a few days before he started East to attend the great university.

While studying political science in Cambridge, Ralph Bunche got a job as clerk and all-around man in a small bookshop whose owner was quite elderly and could not see very well. However, he liked his young employee's knowledge and courtesy a great deal. But one day some customers must have complained about being served by a colored man. The old proprietor squinted at Ralph's golden skin and finally asked him if he were a Negro. When Ralph said he was, the old man replied that he had never given his racial background a thought one way or another and did not care, anyhow, so just keep on working there. This old New England gentleman remained one of his best friends. In 1928 Ralph Bunche received a Master of Arts degree from Harvard and, from among the several teaching posts he was offered, accepted a position to set up a department of political science at Howard University in Washington, D. C.

Ralph Bunche found Washington more prejudiced in its racial attitudes than any city he had ever known. He said later that he spent most of his free time in the Library of Congress because it was one of the few places a Negro in Washington could go without segregation—since all the downtown theaters, movies, restaurants, and hotels were then closed to colored people. As a political scientist Bunche was interested in getting at the roots of the American race problem, and he found the national capital a good place to gather data. So the twenty-four-year-old teacher was kept busy there—but not too busy to fall in love with a beautiful girl in one of his classes. In 1930 there was a June wedding and the Bunches began to plan a house in Washington. Another year of graduate study at Harvard followed. Then, moving up the academic scale, Bunche became an assistant professor, then Assistant to the President of Howard University. In 1931 a Rosenwald Fellowship enabled him to go to Europe and Africa to gather first-hand material on social problems for his doctorate. And in 1934, at Harvard University, he was made a Ph.D. in political science. Two years later he became a full professor at Howard. Two daughters were born, and Ralph settled down to a life of teaching in Washington. But not for long. By now he was becoming famous as an expert in race relations, and many requests for his services, skill, and information came to him.

In 1936 Dr. Bunche was co-director of the Institute of Race Relations at Swarthmore College. In 1941 the great Swedish sociologist, Gunnar Myrdal, backed by the Carnegie Foundation, was asked to make a comprehensive study of Negro-white relations in the United States. The first person he thought of engaging as one of his chief assistants was Ralph Bunche. Howard University then granted Dr. Bunche a leave of absence and, with Myrdal and others of his staff, he made extended field trips into the South, surveying con-

Ralph Bunche

ditions and asking thousands of questions of Negroes and whites. Myrdal and his staff several times were threatened with violence in more than one backward community that did not wish its anti-Negro practices recorded. But, in the end, the great work, *An American Dilemma,* resulted. For this Bunche prepared more than three thousand pages of detailed reports.

When the Second World War broke out, Bunche was barred from military service by the deafness in one ear. The government, however requisitioned him for the Office of Strategic Services, and he was put in charge of research on Africa and other colonial areas in which the Allies had military interests. General Bill Donovan called Bunche "a walking colonial institute" since he knew so much that was helpful in planning African bases for an invasion of Hitler's Europe. He could give the general staffs information on African tribal attitudes toward the war, local social customs, native feelings concerning white people, how they would react to airbases in their midst, and much else that was of great value in military strategy. So successfully did Ralph Bunche do this job that in 1944 the State Department selected him for the Associate Chief of the Division of Dependent Territories. Some members of the State Department objected to a Negro having so important a job. But Secretary of State Cordell Hull fought it through and personally phoned Dr. Bunche to inform him of the confirmation of the appointment. Dr. Bunche then became the first Negro in American history to be in full charge of an office in the State Department.

At the end of the war, Ralph Bunche was assigned by the government as a consultant at the Dumbarton Oaks Conference which was concerned with the economic rebuilding of a war-torn world. When the first meetings to draft a charter for the formation of the United Nations were held at San Francisco, Ralph Bunche was there as advisor to Commander Harold Stassen. Bunche prepared voluminous memoranda for these conferences, particularly concerning the proposed trusteeships of the former colonies of our enemies in the Near East, Africa, and the Pacific. Many of Bunche's recommendations became a part of the Charter of the United Nations, and diplomats of all the governments of the world became aware of this brilliant young Negro in Washington.

Famous American Negroes

In rapid succession various commissions and appointments followed. Bunche was with the United States delegation to the International Labor Conference at Paris in 1945. He was the presidential appointee to the Caribbean Commission in 1946. He was U. S. Commissioner to the West Indian Conference in the Virgin Islands. He went to various United Nations sessions in London and Paris. And in 1947 he was asked by Trygve Lie, then United Nations Secretary-General, to fly to Palestine to aid the United Nations Special Committee in negotiating peace between the Arabs and the Jews. When Count Folke Bernadotte was appointed official Mediator, Ralph Bunche was made chief aid to Bernadotte and the head of his Secretariat. With the Swedish diplomat he toured the battlefields of the Holy Land, their cars bearing the peace flag of the United Nations. They held innumerable meetings with both sides, seeking to end the bloodshed and rancor between the two religious groups who had both occupied the same soil for centuries. Their U. N. cars were often fired upon by snipers. Once the chauffeur who was driving Dr. Bunche was killed at the wheel, and only by quick action did Bunche keep the car from overturning in a ditch. Certainly his Palestine assignment was very dangerous and, so it seemed then, an almost hopeless task. The national, racial, and religious problems involved were extremely complicated ones. Then, to make matters worse, Count Bernadotte was assassinated and several of his staff killed or wounded when their car was ambushed on the road by terrorists. Immediately, the United Nations cabled Ralph Bunche to take over as Acting-Mediator in the murdered Count's place.

It was under such conditions of terror that Dr. Bunche began his personal efforts to bring the Jews and the Arabs to iron out, by conferences rather than bullets, the difficulties between them. Almost nobody believed he could succeed. But he called both Arab and Jew to the Greek Island of Rhodes for a series of talks at the Hotel des Roses. At first the belligerents would not even speak to each other. But by sheer patience, good will, and tact, Ralph Bunche was finally able to bring them together for informal conversations, and, sometimes, a few at a time, for late suppers in his own suite of rooms. At last, he was able to achieve formal meetings to consider a truce. For forty-two days they met, with a crisis coming up almost every day. Sleeping

Ralph Bunche

sometimes only three or four hours a night, Ralph Bunche almost exhausted his large staff of advisors and secretaries. But finally he arrived at a partial truce. Then about a month later he secured a cease-fire agreement. But it still took almost another month to get a formally signed armistice. The day before Bunche, the other United Nations negotiators working with him, the Jews, and the Arabs, stayed up in conference all night long—a session of almost twenty-four hours—to finally secure the signing of a peace that was hailed around the world. The leader of the Israeli delegation said that morning that Bunche had earned the gratitude of all humanity. And the Sheik heading the Arab group called him one of the greatest men on earth. Evidently the committee in charge of granting the world's most distinguished award agreed, for they voted him the Nobel Peace Prize in 1950.

Now, as Director of the Trusteeship Division of the United Nations, the ample talents and great scholarship which Ralph Bunche possesses find a wide field of usefulness. His efforts are concerned with the problems of millions of people in various parts of the world whose lands have not yet attained self-government. Dr. Bunche believes that their problems can be solved, and he has written that he has great faith in "the kind of world the United Nations is working incessantly to bring about: a world at peace; a world in which there is full respect for human rights and fundamental freedoms for all without distinction as to race, sex, language, or religion; a world in which all men shall walk together as equals and with dignity."

MARIAN ANDERSON

MARIAN ANDERSON

Famous Concert Singer

W<small>HEN</small> Marian Anderson was born in a little red brick house in Philadelphia, a famous group of Negro singers, the Fisk Jubilee Singers, had already carried the spirituals all over Europe. And a colored woman billed as "Black Patti" had become famous on variety programs as a singer of both folk songs and the classics. Both Negro and white minstrels had popularized American songs. The all-Negro musical comedies of Bert Williams and George Walker had been successful on Broadway. But no well-trained colored singers performing the great songs of Schubert, Handel, and the other masters, or the arias from famous operas, had become successful on the concert stage. And most people thought of Negro vocalists only in connection with spirituals. Roland Hayes and Marian Anderson were the first to become famous enough to break this stereotype.

Marian Anderson's mother was a staunch church worker who loved to croon the hymns of her faith about the house, as did the aunt who came to live with them when Marian's father died. Both parents were from Virginia. Marian's mother had been a school teacher there, and her father a farm boy. Shortly after they moved to Philadelphia where three daughters were born, the father died, and the mother went to work at Wanamaker's department store. But she saw to it that her children attended school and church regularly. The father had been an usher in the Union Baptist Church, so the congregation took an interest in his three little girls. Marian was the oldest and, before she was eight, singing in the Sunday school choir, she had already learned a great many hymns and spirituals by heart.

One day Marian saw an old violin in a pawnshop window marked $3.45.

She set her mind on that violin, and began to save the nickels and dimes neighbors would give her for scrubbing their white front steps—the kind of stone steps so characteristic of Philadelphia and Baltimore houses—until she had $3.00. The pawnshop man let her take the violin at a reduced price. Marian never became very good on the violin. A few years later her mother bought a piano, so the child forgot all about it in favor of their newer instrument. By that time, too, her unusual singing voice had attracted the attention of her choir master, and at the age of fourteen she was promoted to a place in the main church choir. There she learned all four parts of all the hymns and anthems and could easily fill in anywhere from bass to soprano.

Sensing that she had exceptional musical talent, some of the church members began to raise money so that she might have singing lessons. But her first teacher, a colored woman, refused to accept any pay for instructing so talented a child. So the church folks put their money into a trust fund called "Marian Anderson's Future," banking it until the time came for her to have advanced training. Meanwhile, Marian attended South Philadelphia High School for Girls and took part in various group concerts, usually doing the solo parts. When she was fifteen she sang a group of songs alone at a Sunday School Convention in Harrisburg and word of her talent began to spread about the state. When she was graduated from high school, the Philadelphia Choral Society, a Negro group, sponsored her further study and secured for her one of the best local teachers. Then in 1925 she journeyed to New York to take part, with three hundred other young singers, in the New York Philharmonic Competitions, where she won first place, and was presented with the orchestra at Lewisohn Stadium.

This appearance was given wide publicity, but very few lucrative engagements came in, so Marian continued to study. A Town Hall concert was arranged for her in New York, but it was unsuccessful. Meanwhile, she kept on singing with various choral groups, and herself gave concerts in churches and at some of the Negro colleges until, in 1930, a Rosenald Fellowship made European study possible. During her first year abroad she made her debut in Berlin. A prominent Scandinavian concert manager read of this concert, but was attracted more by the name, *Anderson,* than by what the

Marian Anderson

critics said about her voice. "Ah," he said, "a Negro singer with a Swedish name! She is bound to be a success in Scandinavia." He sent two of his friends to Germany to hear her, one of them being Kosti Vehanen who shortly became her accompanist and remained with her for many years.

Sure enough, Marian Anderson did become a great success in the Scandinavian countries, where she learned to sing in both Finnish and Swedish, and her first concert tour of Europe became a critical triumph. When she came back home to America, she gave several programs and appeared as soloist with the famous Hall Johnson Choir, but without financial success. However, the Scandinavian people, who had fallen in love with her, kept asking her to come back there. So, in 1933, she went again to Europe for 142 concerts in Norway, Sweden, Denmark, and Finland. She was decorated by the King of Denmark and the King of Sweden. Sibelius dedicated a song to her. And the following spring she made her debut in Paris where she was so well received that she had to give three concerts that season at the Salle Gaveau. Great successes followed in all the European capitals. In 1935 the famous conductor, Arturo Toscanini, listened to her sing at Salzburg. He said, "What I heard today one is privileged to hear only once in a hundred years." It was in Europe that Marian Anderson began to be acclaimed by critics as "the greatest singer in the world."

When Marian Anderson again returned to America, she was a seasoned artist. News of her tremendous European successes had preceded her, so a big New York concert was planned. But a few days before she arrived at New York, in a storm on the liner crossing the Atlantic, Marian fell and broke her ankle. She refused to allow this to interfere with her concert, however, nor did she even want people to know about it. She wore a very long evening gown that night so that no one could see the plaster cast on her leg. She propped herself in a curve of the piano before the curtains parted, and gave her New York concert standing on one foot! The next day Howard Taubman wrote enthusiastically in *The New York Times*:

"Marian Anderson has returned to her native land one of the great singers of our time. . . . There is no doubt of it, she was mistress of all she surveyed. . . . It was music making that probed too deep for words."

133

Famous American Negroes

A Coast to Coast American tour followed. And, from that season on, Marian Anderson has been one of our country's favorite singers, rated, according to *Variety,* among the top ten of the concert stage who earn over $100,000 a year. Miss Anderson has sung with the great symphony orchestras, and appeared on all the major radio and television networks many times, being a particular favorite with the millions of listeners to the Ford Hour. During the years she has returned often to Europe for concerts, and among the numerous honors accorded her abroad was a request for a command performance before the King and Queen of England, and a decoration from the government of Finland. Her concerts in South America and Asia have been as successful as those elsewhere. Since 1935 she has averaged over one hundred programs a year in cities as far apart as Vienna, Buenos Aires, Moscow, and Tokyo. Her recordings have sold millions of copies around the world. She has been invited more than once to sing at the White House. She has appeared in concert at the Paris Opera and at the Metropolitan Opera House in New York. Several colleges have granted her honorary degrees, and in 1944 Smith College made her a Doctor of Music.

In spite of all this, as a Negro, Marian Anderson has not been immune from those aspects of racial segregation which affect most travelling artists of color in the United States. In his book, *Marian Anderson,* her longtime accompanist, Vehanen, tells of hotel accommodations being denied her, and service in dining rooms often refused. Once after a concert in a Southern city, Vehanen writes that some white friends drove Marian to the railroad station and took her into the main waiting room. But a policeman ran them out, since Negroes were not allowed in that part of the station. Then they went into the smaller waiting room marked, COLORED. But again they were ejected, because *white* people were not permitted in the cubby hole allotted to Negroes. So they all had to stand on the platform until the train arrived.

The most dramatic incident of prejudice in all Marian Anderson's career occurred in 1939 when the Daughters of the American Revolution, who own Constitution Hall in Washington, refused to allow her to sing there. The newspapers headlined this and many Americans were outraged. In protest a committee of prominent people, including a number of great artists and

Marian Anderson

distinguished figures in the government, was formed. Through the efforts of this committee, Marian Anderson sang in Washington, anyway—before the statue of Abraham Lincoln—to one of the largest crowds ever to hear a singer at one time in the history of the world. Seventy-five-thousand people stood in the open air on a cold clear Easter Sunday afternoon to hear her. And millions more listened to Marian Anderson that day over the radio or heard her in the newsreels that recorded the event. Harold Ickes, then Secretary of the Interior, presented Miss Anderson to that enormous audience standing in the plaza to pay honor, as he said, not only to a great singer, but to the basic ideals of democracy and equality.

In 1943 Marian Anderson married Orpheus H. Fisher, an architect, and settled down—between tours—in a beautiful country house in Connecticut where she rehearses new songs to add to her already vast repertoire. Sometimes her neighbors across the fields can hear the rich warm voice that covers three octaves singing in English, French, Finnish, or German. And sometimes they hear in the New England air that old Negro spiritual, "Honor, honor unto the dying Lamb. . . ."

Friends say that Marian Anderson has invested her money in real estate and in government bonds. Certainly, throughout her career, she has lived very simply, traveled without a maid or secretary, and carried her own sewing machine along by train, ship, or plane to mend her gowns. When in 1941 in Philadelphia she was awarded the coveted Bok Award for outstanding public service, the $10,000 that came with the medallion she used to establish a trust fund for "talented American artists without regard to race or creed." Now, each year from this fund promising young musicians receive scholarships.

JACKIE ROBINSON

JACKIE ROBINSON

First Negro in Big League Baseball

Born 1919—

CAIRO IS A village in southern Georgia not far from the Florida state line. There, to a poor sharecropping family, on January 31, 1919, John Roosevelt Robinson was born, the youngest of five children. His father died before the boy could learn to remember him, leaving the mother as the only support for her children. So, when little John Roosevelt was about fourteen months old, and the other youngsters ranged from two-and-a-half to ten, Mrs. Mollie Robinson set out with her brood for California where she had heard that times were better and there were good non-segreated schools for children. Mrs. Robinson had a half brother in Pasadena who had promised them a place to stay. The children called him Uncle Burton, and he became like a father to them all, four boys and a girl, sharing with them his two rooms.

They nicknamed the baby Jackie and in the California sunshine he grew strong and healthy. Mrs. Robinson worked sometimes as a domestic servant and sometimes as a laundress, and did her best to keep the children clean and in school. But, with so many, they often did not have quite enough to eat, so little Jackie remembers with particular affection one kind teacher who would sometimes share her lunch with him. And sometimes he bought a nickel bag of peanuts and ate not only the nuts, but the shells, to help fill him up. His wonderful mother washed and ironed their clothes on Saturday night so she might send them neatly dressed to Sunday school and, in every way, she did all that she could to bring them up decently. But she was often away from home working to buy them clothes and food and pay rent on the larger house to which they moved. It was not easy for one woman alone to make enough money to buy shoes for ten active little feet, and keep the pots well filled on the stove, too. It was not her fault if her income did not stretch as far as her love.

The depression of the 1930's made times hard indeed. Still all five of Mollie Robinson's children continued to attend either the Cleveland Elementary School or the Muir Technical High School where Jackie's brother, Mack, became a champion sprinter and broad jumper. Sturdy little Jackie himself was a member of the grammar school soccer team that beat all comers. These two boys of the Robinson family were early known as fine young athletes.

When Jackie was fourteen he entered high school and, following his brother's footsteps there, he became a star athlete, going out for football, basketball, baseball, and track, and playing on all teams. When he was graduated from Muir he was a four-letter man, almost six feet tall, weighing 175 pounds, and still developing. The coaches at Pasadena Junior College welcomed him with open arms, and there he continued to make a distinguished athletic record. In track he set a new junior college broad jump record of 25 feet 6 1/3 inches. In baseball he led the conference with a batting average of .460. And in a single basketball game he broke the individual points record by scoring 28 points in a single game. He was a popular student, good humored, praised for his fair sportsmanship, and not conceited. Since the third grade when he began to play so well on his elementary school soccer team, Jackie had been accustomed to the cheers of his classmates on the sidelines, so he took his junior college triumphs in stride, as nothing unusual at all.

When the two years of junior college were up in 1938, Jackie went to the University of California at Los Angeles to major in Physical Education, riding by bus every morning for more than an hour from Pasadena to the campus. Meanwhile, his brother Mack had taken part in the 1936 Olympic Games at Berlin, finishing second only to Jesse Owens in the 200 meters dash, and setting a new record for that distance at Paris a few weeks later. Jackie adored big brother Mack and continued to try to emulate him. Right away he went out for football at UCLA, and his first season on the team he became a star. As a quarterback in the first big game of the season against the Uni-

Jackie Robinson

versity of Washington, Jackie made the gains that broke a tie score and won the game for UCLA. Before a sprained ankle halted his progress toward the end of the season, Jackie had scored four touchdowns and kicked two points after touchdowns to account for 26 points of his team's total 127. Every time he had gotten the ball he had averaged 12 yards a carry. Out of 14 ball-carryings, he had averaged over 20 yards each time, which set a new record in college football. So Jackie's name became known far and wide as an exceptional gridiron player.

In basketball the same thing happened. Jackie starred in the twelve games that he played, and became the top point scorer that season in the Pacific Coast Conference with 148 points. In track he broke the conference broad jump record, and was a member of the West Coast team that defeated the Big Ten at Northwestern. Then he fell in love with a girl on the campus and began to look forward to marriage. About that time Uncle Burton became ill, and it seemed unfair to Jackie to let his mother carry the whole financial burden of their household alone. So in the spring of 1941 during his second and final year at UCLA, Jackie quit college and went to work at a government Civilian Conservation Corp camp as an athletic director.

When the government camp closed, an offer came to Jackie to play in the *Chicago Tribune* All-Star charity football game at Soldier's Field in Chicago. From this came an engagement in professional football with the Los Angeles Bulldogs at a very good salary. But just after a series of games in Honolulu, while Jackie was on the boat coming home, Pearl Harbor was bombed, and America entered the Second World War. Jackie went into the army. He was sent to Fort Riley, Kansas, where Joe Louis, too, was stationed, and the two became friends. Assigned to a calvary unit, Jackie spent his time vaccinating horses. But when his basic training was over, he applied for officers' school. In 1943 he was commissioned a second lieutenant and was sent to the 761st Tank Battalion at Camp Hood, Texas, where, within a few months his commanding officer commended Robinson for the fine record he made in the training of his men. But his old football injury, the torn ankle, began bothering him and, after thirty-one months service, Jackie was honorably discharged from the army.

Famous American Negroes

The minister of his mother's church in Pasadena had become the President of a small Negro college, Samuel Houston, in Austin, Texas. So when Jackie got home from the army he found a letter offering him the position of athletic director on the faculty there. Since he had enjoyed working with young men in the C.C.C. camp, he welcomed this job with interest. But he did not stay there long for the salary was very low, and at home Uncle Burton was by now bed-ridden, which made it difficult for his mother to continue to go out to work. When the Kansas City Monarchs, a team in the Negro American Base-ball League, offered him $400.00 a month as a short stop, Jackie accepted, and began a barnstorming tour from South to North with them. This meant bad hotels, Jim Crow meals, long dusty bus trips, and sometimes six or seven games a week with no rest. But Jackie could send money home and still save something to get married. In 1946 he and Rachel Isum, the girl he had met in college, marched happily to the altar together.

When Clyde Sukeforth, a scout for the Brooklyn Dodgers Baseball Team, asked Jackie one late afternoon following a game in Chicago, to come to New York to see Branch Rickey, President of the Dodgers, Jackie was almost rude. Whether he frowned or laughed in Sukeforth's face is not clear. But any rate, like most Negro players, he did not like to be "kidded" about the pos-sibilities of playing in the major leagues. To Negroes the "great American sport" was then the "great American *white* sport," since they were barred from teams in the big leagues. Even such really exceptional ball players as Satchel Paige and Josh Gibson had never had a chance to play with the famous major league teams, only with barnstorming Negro outfits. So Jackie thought Clyde Sukeforth was joking the day he asked him to take a train East to talk with the head of the Brooklyn Dodgers. Finally the scout was able to persuade Robinson that he was on the level, and that he had been watching his playing for some time. Having an injured shoulder, Jackie could take a few days off without being fined, so he went to Brooklyn. The rest is history.

World War II had brought about many changes for the better in America's racial climate. The government had ordered war industries opened to skilled Negro workers after A. Philip Randolph's threatened March-on-Washington. The pressure of Negro and white liberals in the National Association for the

142

Jackie Robinson

Advancement of Colored People and other organizations had helped break down the bars of segregation in the Marines, the Air Force, and other branches of the service where Negroes had previously not been permitted to serve. A wave of equality for the darker peoples of the world was sweeping around the earth from India and the Far East to the United Nations. Negro Americans, too, backed by the finest sentiments of many leading Americans in and out of government, were calling for the end of the color bar in voting, housing, education—and baseball. Now, if ever, was the time to begin to admit Negro players to the major leagues. Then, too, the war had robbed the leagues of many of their best players. They were in need of good men. Of the younger Negro athletes, Jackie was certainly a great ball player, a college-trained man, and a gentleman. Branch Rickey completed arrangements for Jackie Robinson to join the Montreal Royals of the International League, a minor league farm team of the Brooklyn Dodgers.

During his first season as second baseman at Montreal Jackie played sensational ball. In his initial game against the Newark Bears he batted out a three-run homer, three singles, stole two bases, slugged in four runs, and scored four times. Montreal won the International League pennant at the end of the season and went on to victory against the Louisville Colonels in the Little World Series. Jackie topped the league with a batting average of .349 and a fielding average of .985. He also led in hits and runs, 155 and 113 respectively, out of 124 games. Despite this record, there was a great deal of opposition inside and outside baseball circles to his being brought into the Dodgers. Some folks said neither the players nor the fans would accept him, and that in cities like St. Louis there would be race riots if Jackie appeared on the diamond. Branch Rickey had to consider all these factors in making up his mind to admit the first Negro player to a big league roster. But on April 10, 1947, Rickey signed Robinson as a member of the Dodgers at a salary of $5,000 a season.

There were no race riots. Box office receipts soared as fans everywhere crowded the stands to see the Dodgers play. And Jackie played brilliantly. He had been asked by Rickey to let his A-1 brand of baseball *alone* answer all slurs, racial jibes, and unfairness that might come up. Most of the fans and most of the players on his own and rival teams treated Jackie fairly. When they didn't, even when someone threw a black cat on the field to taunt him, those first two seasons Robinson kept his head, kept on playing great ball, and steadily built up a reputation as the most valuable player in the National League, whose batting champion he became in 1949. His very first season the Dodgers won the pennant, and Robinson himself was named "The Rookie of the Year." For a time the newspapers devoted more space to Jackie Robinson than to any other sports personality in the United States. And, as Joe Louis had been in the ring, so Jackie Robinson became a symbol to millions in America of the progress which young Negroes in the postwar world might make.

The Dodgers gave Robinson a chance to play before the millions of fans who go to the big league parks. Once the racial ice was broken, other teams followed the Dodgers' example, by employing Negro players. Shortly the Dodgers themselves had signed Don Newcombe, Roy Campanella, and Dan Bankhead. And the "great American sport" had become in truth an *American* sport. Jackie Robinson blazed a trail for democracy when for the first time he went to bat at Ebbetts Field.

INDEX

145

Index

Index